The Secret of
FAMILY
HAPPINESS

PUBLISHERS

WATCHTOWER BIBLE AND TRACT SOCIETY OF NEW YORK, INC.

INTERNATIONAL BIBLE STUDENTS ASSOCIATION

BROOKLYN, NEW YORK, U.S.A.

FIRST PRINTING IN ENGLISH:

5,000,000 COPIES

UNLESS OTHERWISE INDICATED,
SCRIPTURE QUOTATIONS ARE FROM THE MODERN-LANGUAGE
NEW WORLD TRANSLATION OF THE HOLY SCRIPTURES—WITH REFERENCES

THE SECRET OF FAMILY HAPPINESS   ENGLISH (*fy*-E)

MADE IN THE UNITED STATES OF AMERICA

CONTENTS

CHAPTER ONE

Is There a Secret of Family Happiness?

THE family is the oldest institution on earth, and it plays a vital role in human society. Throughout history, strong families have helped to make strong societies. The family is the best arrangement for bringing up children to be mature adults.

² A happy family is a haven of safety and security. Envision the ideal family for a moment. During their evening meal, caring parents sit with their children and discuss the events of the day. Children chatter excitedly as they tell their father and mother about what happened at school. The relaxing time spent

---

1. Why are strong families important in human society?
2-5. (a) Describe the security a child feels in a happy family. (b) What problems are reported in some families?

together refreshes everyone for another day in the world outside.

³ In a happy family, a child knows that his father and mother will care for him when he gets sick, perhaps taking turns at his bedside through the night. He knows that he can go to his mother or father with the problems of his young life and get advice and support. Yes, the child feels safe, no matter how trouble-filled the outside world may be.

⁴ When children grow up, they usually get married and have a family of their own. "A person realizes how indebted he is to his parents when he has a child of his own," says an Oriental proverb. With a deep sense of gratitude and love, the grown children try to make their own families happy, and they also care for their now aging parents, who delight in the company of the grandchildren.

⁵ Perhaps at this point you are thinking: 'Well, I love my family, but it is not like the one just described. My spouse and I work different schedules and hardly see each other. We talk mostly about money problems.' Or do you say, 'My children and grandchildren live in another town, and I never get to see them'? Yes, for reasons often beyond the control of those involved, much family life is less than ideal. Still, some lead happy family lives. How? Is there a secret of family happiness? The answer is yes. But before discussing what it is, we should answer an important question.

WHAT IS A FAMILY?

⁶ In Western lands, most families consist of a father, a mother, and children. Grandparents may live

---

6. What kind of families will be discussed in this book?

in their own households as long as they can. While contact is kept up with more-distant relatives, duties toward these are limited. Basically, this is the family that we will discuss in this book. However, other families have become increasingly common in recent years—the single-parent family, the stepfamily, and the family whose parents are not living together for one reason or another.

[7] Common in some cultures is the extended family. In this arrangement, if possible, grandparents are routinely looked after by their children, and close ties and responsibilities extend to distant relatives. For instance, family members may help to support, raise, and even pay for the education of their nieces, nephews, or more-distant relatives. The principles to be discussed in this publication apply also to extended families.

THE FAMILY UNDER STRESS

[8] Today the family is changing—sad to say, not for the better. An example is seen in India, where a wife may live with the family of her husband and work in the home under the direction of her in-laws. Nowadays, though, it is not uncommon for Indian wives to seek employment outside the home. Yet they are apparently still expected to fulfill their traditional roles in the home. The question raised in many lands is, Compared with other members of the family, how much work should a woman with an outside job be expected to do in the home?

[9] In Oriental societies, strong extended-family ties are traditional. However, under the influence of

---

7. What is the extended family?
8, 9. What problems in some lands show that the family is changing?

Western-style individualism and the stress of economic problems, the traditional extended family is weakening. Many, therefore, view care of aged family members as a burden rather than as a duty or a privilege. Some elderly parents are abused. Indeed, abuse and neglect of the aged are found in many countries today.

[10] Divorce is becoming increasingly common. In Spain the divorce rate rose to 1 out of 8 marriages by the beginning of the final decade of the 20th century—a big jump from 1 out of 100 just 25 years before. Britain, with reportedly the highest divorce rate in Europe (4 out of 10 marriages are expected to fail), has seen a surge in the number of single-parent families.

[11] Many in Germany seem to be abandoning the traditional family altogether. The 1990's saw 35 percent of all German households made up of a single person and 31 percent made up of just two individuals. The French too are marrying less often, and those who do marry divorce more often and earlier than used to be the case. Growing numbers prefer to live together without the responsibilities of marriage. Comparable trends are seen worldwide.

[12] What of children? In the United States and many other lands, more and more are born out of wedlock, some to young teenagers. Many teenage girls have a number of children from different fathers. Reports from around the world tell of millions of homeless children roaming the streets; many are

---

10, 11. What facts show that the family is changing in European lands?

12. How do children suffer because of changes in the modern family?

escaping from abusive homes or are cast out by families that can no longer support them.

¹³ Yes, the family is in crisis. In addition to what has already been mentioned, teenage rebellion, child abuse, spousal violence, alcoholism, and other devastating problems rob many families of happiness. For a great number of children and adults, the family is far from being a haven.

¹⁴ Why the family crisis? Some blame the present-day family crisis on the entry of women into the workplace. Others point to today's moral breakdown. And additional causes are cited. Almost two thousand years ago, a well-known lawyer foretold that many pressures would afflict the family, when he wrote: "In the last days critical times hard to deal with will be here. For men will be lovers of themselves, lovers of money, self-assuming, haughty, blasphemers, disobedient to parents, unthankful, disloyal, having no natural affection, not open to any agreement, slanderers, without self-control, fierce, without love of goodness, betrayers, headstrong, puffed up with pride, lovers of pleasures rather than lovers of God." (2 Timothy 3:1-4) Who would doubt that these words are being fulfilled today? In a world with conditions such as these, is it any wonder that many families are in crisis?

THE SECRET OF FAMILY HAPPINESS

¹⁵ Counsel on how to achieve happiness in the

---

13. What widespread problems rob families of happiness?
14. (a) According to some, what are the causes of the family crisis? (b) How did a first-century lawyer describe today's world, and what influence has the fulfillment of his words had on family life?
15-17. In this book, what authority will be pointed to as holding the secret of family happiness?

family is offered from all sides. In the West, a never-ending stream of self-help books and magazines offer advice. The problem is that human counselors contradict one another, and what is fashionable counsel today may be viewed as unworkable tomorrow.

[16] Where, then, can we look for reliable family guidance? Well, would you look to a book completed some 1,900 years ago? Or would you feel that a book like this must be hopelessly out-of-date? The truth is, the real secret of family happiness is found in just such a source.

[17] That source is the Bible. According to all the evidence, it was inspired by God himself. In the Bible we find the following statement: "All Scripture is inspired of God and beneficial for teaching, for reproving, for setting things straight, for disciplining in righteousness." (2 Timothy 3:16) In this publication we will encourage you to consider how the Bible can help you to 'set things straight' when handling the stresses and problems facing families today.

[18] If you are inclined to dismiss the possibility that the Bible can help to make families happy, consider this: The One who inspired the Bible is the Originator of the marriage arrangement. (Genesis 2:18-25) The Bible says that his name is Jehovah. (Psalm 83:18) He is the Creator and 'the Father, to whom every family owes its name.' (Ephesians 3:14, 15) Jehovah has observed family life since mankind's beginning. He knows the problems that can arise and has given counsel for solving them. Throughout history, those who sincerely applied Bible principles in their family life found greater happiness.

---

18. Why is it reasonable to accept the Bible as an authority in marriage counseling?

FAMILY HAPPINESS

[19] For example, a housewife in Indonesia was a compulsive gambler. For years she neglected her three children and regularly quarreled with her husband. Then she started to study the Bible. Gradually the woman came to believe what the Bible said. When she applied its counsel, she became a better wife. Her efforts, based on Bible principles, brought happiness to her entire family.

[20] A housewife in Spain says: "We had been married only a year when we began to have serious problems." She and her husband did not have much in common, and they spoke little except when they were arguing. Despite having a young daughter, they decided to get a legal separation. Before that happened, though, they were encouraged to look into the Bible. They studied its counsel for married men and women and began to apply it. Before long, they could communicate peacefully, and their small family was happily united.

[21] The Bible helps older people too. For instance, consider the experience of a certain Japanese couple. The husband was short-tempered and sometimes violent. First, the couple's daughters began to study the Bible, despite their parents' opposition. Then, the husband joined his daughters, but the wife continued to object. Over the years, however, she noticed the good effect of Bible principles on her family. Her daughters took good care of her, and her husband became much milder. Such changes moved the woman to look into the Bible for herself, and it had the same good effect on her. This elderly

---

19-21. What modern experiences show the power of the Bible to solve marriage problems?

lady repeatedly said: "We became a real married couple."

²² These individuals are among the great many who have learned the secret of family happiness. They have accepted the Bible's counsel and have applied it. True, they live in the same violent, immoral, economically stressed world as everyone else. Moreover, they are imperfect, but they find happiness in trying to do the will of the Originator of the family arrangement. As the Bible says, Jehovah God is "the One teaching you to benefit yourself, the One causing you to tread in the way in which you should walk."—Isaiah 48:17.

²³ Although the Bible was completed almost two thousand years ago, its counsel is truly up-to-date. Further, it was written for *all* people. The Bible is not an American or a Western book. Jehovah "made out of one man every nation of men," and He knows the makeup of humans everywhere. (Acts 17:26) Bible principles work for everyone. If you apply them, you too will come to know the secret of family happiness.

22, 23. How does the Bible help people of all national backgrounds to find happiness in their family life?

CAN YOU ANSWER THESE QUESTIONS?

What is happening to the family today?
—2 Timothy 3:1-4.

Who originated the family arrangement?
—Ephesians 3:14, 15.

What is the secret of family happiness?
—Isaiah 48:17.

FAMILY HAPPINESS

CHAPTER TWO

Preparing for a Successful Marriage

CONSTRUCTING a building requires careful preparation. Before the foundation is laid, land must be acquired and plans drawn up. However, something else is vital. Jesus said: "Who of you that wants to build a tower does not first sit down and calculate the expense, to see if he has enough to complete it?"—Luke 14:28.

² What is true of constructing a building also applies to constructing a successful marriage. Many say: "I want to get married." But how many stop

---

1, 2. (a) How did Jesus stress the importance of planning? (b) In what field particularly is planning vital?

to consider the cost? While the Bible speaks favorably of marriage, it also draws attention to the challenges that marriage presents. (Proverbs 18:22; 1 Corinthians 7:28) Therefore, those contemplating marriage need to have a realistic view of both the blessings and the costs of being married.

³ The Bible can help. Its counsel is inspired by the Originator of marriage, Jehovah God. (Ephesians 3:14, 15; 2 Timothy 3:16) Using the principles found in this ancient yet very up-to-date guidebook, let us determine (1) How can a person tell whether he or she is ready for marriage? (2) What should be looked for in a mate? and (3) How can courtship be kept honorable?

ARE YOU READY FOR MARRIAGE?

⁴ Constructing a building may be expensive, but caring for its long-term maintenance is costly as well. It is similar with marriage. Getting married seems challenging enough; however, maintaining a marital relationship year after year must also be considered. What does maintaining such a relationship entail? A vital factor is a wholehearted commitment. Here is how the Bible describes the marriage relationship: "A man will leave his father and his mother and he must stick to his wife and they must become one flesh." (Genesis 2:24) Jesus Christ gave the only Scriptural basis for divorce with the possibility of remarriage—"fornication," that is, illicit sex relations outside the marriage.

---

3. Why is the Bible a valuable aid to those planning for marriage, and what three questions will it help us to answer?
4. What is a vital factor in maintaining a successful marriage, and why?

(Matthew 19:9) If you are contemplating marriage, bear these Scriptural standards in mind. If you are not ready for this solemn commitment, then you are not ready for marriage.—Deuteronomy 23:21; Ecclesiastes 5:4, 5.

⁵ The idea of a solemn commitment frightens many. "Knowing that the two of us were stuck together for life made me feel pushed into a corner, closed in, totally confined," confessed one young man. But if you really love the person you intend to marry, commitment will not seem like a burden. Instead, it will be viewed as a source of security. The sense of commitment implied in marriage will make a couple want to stay together through good times and bad and to be supportive of each other come what may. The Christian apostle Paul wrote that true love "bears all things" and "endures all things." (1 Corinthians 13:4, 7) "The commitment of marriage makes me feel more secure," says one woman. "I love the comfort of having admitted to ourselves and the world that we intend to stick together."—Ecclesiastes 4:9-12.

⁶ Living up to such a commitment requires maturity. Thus, Paul counsels that Christians do better not to marry until they are "past the bloom of youth," the period when sexual feelings run strong and can distort one's judgment. (1 Corinthians 7:36) Young people change rapidly as they grow up. Many who marry when very young find that after just a few years their needs and desires, as well as

5. Although the solemn commitment of marriage frightens some, why should it rather be highly valued by those intending to marry?
6. Why is it best not to rush into marriage at a young age?

those of their mate, have changed. Statistics reveal that teenagers who marry are much more likely to be unhappy and seek divorce than those who wait a little longer. So do not rush into marriage. Some years spent living as a young, single adult can give you precious experience that will make you more mature and better qualified to be a suitable mate. Waiting to get married can also help you to understand yourself better—a necessity if you are to develop a successful relationship in your marriage.

KNOW YOURSELF FIRST

[7] Do you find it easy to list the qualities you want in a mate? Most do. However, what about your own qualities? What traits do you have that will help you contribute to a successful marriage? What type of husband or wife will you be? For example, do you freely admit your mistakes and accept advice, or are you always defensive when corrected? Are you generally cheerful and optimistic, or do you tend to be gloomy, frequently complaining? (Proverbs 8:33; 15:15) Remember, marriage will not change your personality. If you are proud, oversensitive, or overly pessimistic when single, you will be the same when married. Since it is difficult to see ourselves the way others see us, why not ask a parent or a trusted friend for frank comments and suggestions? If you learn of changes that could be made, work on these before taking steps to marry.

[8] The Bible encourages us to let God's holy spirit

---

7. Why should those planning to get married examine themselves first?

8-10. What counsel does the Bible give that will help an individual to prepare for marriage?

CUSTOMS AND THE BIBLE

Bride-Price and Dowry: In some lands the groom's family is expected to give money to the bride's family (bride-price). In others, the bride's family gives money to the groom's (dowry). There may be nothing wrong with these customs as long as they are legal. (Romans 13:1) However, in either case, the receiving family should avoid greedily demanding more money or goods than is reasonable. (Proverbs 20:21; 1 Corinthians 6:10) Further, the paying of bride-price should never be construed to imply that a wife is simply purchased property; nor should a husband feel that his only responsibility toward his wife and his in-laws is a financial one.

Polygamy: Some cultures allow a man to take more than one wife. In such an atmosphere, the man may become an overlord rather than a husband and father. Furthermore, polygamous marriage often fosters competition among wives. For Christians, the Bible allows only singleness or monogamy.—1 Corinthians 7:2.

Trial Marriage: Many couples claim that living together before marriage will help them test out their compatibility. Yet, trial marriage does not test one of the most crucial elements of marriage —commitment. No arrangement other than marriage offers the same degree of protection and security to all parties—including any children that may result from the union. In the eyes of Jehovah God, living together consensually without the benefit of marriage is fornication.—1 Corinthians 6:18; Hebrews 13:4.

work in us, producing qualities such as "love, joy, peace, long-suffering, kindness, goodness, faith, mildness, self-control." It also tells us to "be made new in the force actuating [our] mind" and to "put on the new personality which was created according to God's will in true righteousness and loyalty." (Galatians 5:22, 23; Ephesians 4:23, 24) Applying this counsel while you are still single will be like depositing money in the bank—something that will prove very valuable in the future, when you do marry.

⁹ For example, if you are a woman, learn to pay more attention to "the secret person of the heart" than you do to your physical appearance. (1 Peter 3:3, 4) Modesty and soundness of mind will help you to have wisdom, a true "crown of beauty." (Proverbs 4:9; 31:10, 30; 1 Timothy 2:9, 10) If you are a man, learn to treat women in a kind and respectful way. (1 Timothy 5:1, 2) While learning to make decisions and shoulder responsibility, learn also to be modest and humble. A domineering attitude will lead to trouble in a marriage.—Proverbs 29:23; Micah 6:8; Ephesians 5:28, 29.

¹⁰ Although making the mind over in these areas is not easy, it is something all Christians should work on. And it will help you to be a better marriage partner.

WHAT TO LOOK FOR IN A MATE

¹¹ Is it customary where you live for a person to choose his or her own marriage mate? If so, how should you proceed if you find someone of the

11, 12. How may two people find out whether or not they are compatible?

While still single, develop qualities, habits, and abilities that will serve you well in marriage

opposite sex attractive? First, ask yourself, 'Is marriage really my intention?' It is cruel to play with another person's emotions by raising false expectations. (Proverbs 13:12) Then, ask yourself, 'Am I in a position to get married?' If the answer to both questions is positive, the steps you take next will vary depending on local custom. In some lands, after observing for a while, you might approach the person and express a desire to get better acquainted. If the response is negative, do not persist to the point of being objectionable. Remember, the other person also has a right to make a decision in the matter. If, however, the response is positive, you may arrange to spend time together in wholesome activities. This will give you an opportunity to see whether marriage to this person would be wise.* What should you look for at this stage?

¹² To answer that question, imagine two musical instruments, perhaps a piano and a guitar. If they are correctly tuned, either one can produce beautiful solo music. Yet, what happens if these instruments are played together? Now they must be in tune with each other. It is similar with you and a prospective mate. Each of you may have worked hard to "tune" your personality traits as individuals. But the question now is: Are you in tune with each other? In other words, are you compatible?

¹³ It is important that both of you have common beliefs and principles. The apostle Paul wrote:

---

* This would apply in lands where dating is considered appropriate for Christians.

13. Why is it very unwise to court someone who does not share your faith?

FAMILY HAPPINESS

"Do not become unevenly yoked with unbelievers." (2 Corinthians 6:14; 1 Corinthians 7:39) Marriage to someone who does not share your faith in God makes it more likely that there will be severe disharmony. On the other hand, a mutual devotion to Jehovah God is the strongest basis for unity. Jehovah wants you to be happy and to enjoy the closest possible bond with the person you marry. He wants you to be bound to Him and to each other by a threefold bond of love.—Ecclesiastes 4:12.

¹⁴ While worshiping God together is the most important aspect of unity, more is involved. To be attuned to each other, you and your prospective mate should have similar goals. What are your goals? For example, how do you both feel about having children? What things have the first place in your life?* (Matthew 6:33) In a truly successful marriage, the couple are good friends and enjoy each other's company. (Proverbs 17:17) For this, they need to have interests in common. It is difficult to sustain a close friendship—much less a marriage—when this is not the case. Still, if your prospective partner enjoys a particular activity, such as hiking, and you do not, does that mean that the two of you should not get married? Not necessarily. Perhaps you share other, more important interests. Moreover, you might give happiness to your prospective partner by sharing in wholesome

---

* Even in the Christian congregation, there may be some who live on the fringes, as it were. Instead of being wholehearted servants of God, they may be influenced by the attitudes and conduct of the world.—John 17:16; James 4:4.

14, 15. Is having the same faith the only aspect of unity in a marriage? Explain.

activities because the other person enjoys them. —Acts 20:35.

¹⁵ Indeed, to a large degree, compatibility is determined by how adaptable both of you are rather than by how identical you are. Instead of asking, "Do we agree on everything?" some better questions might be: "What happens when we disagree? Can we discuss matters calmly, according each other respect and dignity? Or do discussions often deteriorate into heated arguments?" (Ephesians 4:29, 31) If you want to get married, be wary of anyone who is proud and opinionated, never willing to compromise, or who constantly demands and schemes to have his or her own way.

FIND OUT BEFOREHAND

¹⁶ In the Christian congregation, those who are entrusted with responsibility are to be "tested as to fitness first." (1 Timothy 3:10) You too can employ this principle. For example, a woman might ask, "What kind of reputation does this man have? Who are his friends? Does he display self-control? How does he treat elderly persons? What kind of family does he come from? How does he interact with them? What is his attitude toward money? Does he abuse alcoholic beverages? Is he temperamental, even violent? What congregation responsibilities does he have, and how does he handle them? Could I deeply respect him?"—Leviticus 19:32; Proverbs 22:29; 31:23; Ephesians 5:3-5, 33; 1 Timothy 5:8; 6:10; Titus 2:6, 7.

¹⁷ A man might ask, "Does this woman display

16, 17. What might a man or a woman look for when considering a prospective marriage mate?

love and respect for God? Is she capable of caring for a home? What will her family expect of us? Is she wise, industrious, thrifty? What does she talk about? Is she genuinely concerned about the welfare of others, or is she self-centered, a busybody? Is she trustworthy? Is she willing to submit to headship, or is she stubborn, perhaps even rebellious?"—Proverbs 31:10-31; Luke 6:45; Ephesians 5:22, 23; 1 Timothy 5:13; 1 Peter 4:15.

[18] Do not forget that you are dealing with an imperfect descendant of Adam, not some idealized hero or heroine out of a romance novel. Everyone has shortcomings, and some of these will have to be overlooked—both yours and those of your prospective partner. (Romans 3:23; James 3:2) Further, a perceived weakness can present an opportunity to grow. For example, suppose during your courtship you have an argument. Consider: Even people who love and respect each other disagree at times. (Compare Genesis 30:2; Acts 15:39.) Could it be that both of you simply need to 'restrain your spirit' a little more and learn how to settle matters more peacefully? (Proverbs 25:28) Does your prospective mate show a desire to improve? Do you? Could you learn to be less sensitive, less touchy? (Ecclesiastes 7:9) Learning to resolve problems can establish a pattern of honest communication that is essential if the two of you do get married.—Colossians 3:13.

[19] What, though, if you notice things that trouble

18. If minor weaknesses are perceived during courtship, what should be borne in mind?
19. What would be a wise course of action if serious problems surface during courtship?

you deeply? Such doubts should be considered carefully. However romantic you may feel or however anxious you may be to get married, do not close your eyes to serious faults. (Proverbs 22:3; Ecclesiastes 2:14) If you have a relationship with someone about whom you have serious reservations, it is wise to discontinue the relationship and to refrain from making a lasting commitment to that person.

KEEP YOUR COURTSHIP HONORABLE

[20] How can you keep your courtship honorable? First, make sure that your moral conduct is above reproach. Where you live, is holding hands, kissing, or embracing considered appropriate behavior for unmarried couples? Even if such expressions of affection are not frowned upon, they should be allowed only when the relationship has reached a point where marriage is definitely planned. Be careful that displays of affection do not escalate into unclean conduct or even fornication. (Ephesians 4:18, 19; compare Song of Solomon 1:2; 2:6; 8:5, 9, 10.) Because the heart is treacherous, both of you would be wise to avoid being isolated in a house, an apartment, a parked automobile, or anywhere else that would give opportunity for wrong conduct. (Jeremiah 17:9) Keeping your courtship morally clean gives clear evidence that you have self-control and that you put unselfish concern for the other person's welfare ahead of your own desires. Most important, a clean courtship will please Jehovah

---

20. How can a courting couple keep their moral conduct above reproach?

God, who commands his servants to abstain from uncleanness and fornication.—Galatians 5:19-21.

[21] Second, an honorable courtship also includes honest communication. As your courtship progresses toward marriage, certain matters will need to be discussed openly. Where will you live? Will both of you work secularly? Do you want to have children? Also, it is only fair to reveal things, perhaps in one's past, that could affect the marriage. These may include major debts or obligations or health matters, such as any serious disease or condition you may have. Since many persons who are infected with HIV (the virus that causes AIDS) show no immediate symptoms, it would not be wrong for an individual or for caring parents to request an AIDS blood test of one who has in the past engaged in sexual promiscuity or was an intravenous drug user. If the test proves positive, the infected person should not pressure the intended mate to continue the relationship if that one now wishes to terminate it. Really, anyone who has engaged in a high-risk life-style would do well to submit voluntarily to an AIDS blood test before beginning a courtship.

LOOKING BEYOND THE WEDDING

[22] During the final months before the marriage, both of you will likely be very busy with arranging for the wedding. You can alleviate much of the

---

21. What honest communication may be needed in order to keep courtship honorable?
22, 23. (a) How could balance be lost when preparing for a wedding? (b) What balanced view should be maintained when considering the wedding and the marriage?

tension by being moderate. An elaborate wedding may please relatives and the community, but it may leave newlyweds and their families physically exhausted and financially drained. Some adherence to local customs is reasonable, but slavish and perhaps competitive conformity can overshadow the meaning of the occasion and may rob you of the joy that you should have. While the feelings of others must be considered, the groom is primarily responsible for deciding what will go on at the wedding feast.—John 2:9.

23 Remember that your wedding lasts just one day, but your marriage lasts a lifetime. Avoid concentrating too much on the act of *getting* married. Instead, look to Jehovah God for guidance, and plan ahead for a life of *being* married. Then you will have prepared well for a successful marriage.

HOW CAN THESE BIBLE PRINCIPLES HELP . . . A PERSON TO PREPARE FOR A SUCCESSFUL MARRIAGE?

A husband and wife
must be committed to each other.
—Genesis 2:24.

The inner person is more important
than external appearance.
—1 Peter 3:3, 4.

"Do not become unevenly yoked."
—2 Corinthians 6:14.

Morally unclean people are alienated from God.
—Ephesians 4:18, 19.

CHAPTER THREE

Two Keys to a Lasting Marriage

WHEN God united the first man and woman in marriage, there was no indication that the union would be only temporary. Adam and Eve were to be together for life. (Genesis 2:24) God's standard for an honorable marriage is the uniting of one male and one female. Only gross sexual immorality on the part of one or both mates provides Scriptural grounds for divorce with the possibility of remarriage.—Matthew 5:32.

[2] Is it possible for two individuals to live together happily for an indefinitely long time? Yes, and the Bible identifies two vital factors, or keys, that help to make this possible. If both the husband and the wife put these to use, they will unlock the door to happiness and many blessings. What are these keys?

THE FIRST KEY

[3] The first key is love. Interestingly, there are different kinds of love identified in the Bible. One is a warm, personal affection for someone, the kind of love that exists between close friends. (John 11:3) Another is the love that grows between family members. (Romans 12:10) A third is the romantic love

---

1, 2. (a) For how long was marriage designed to last? (b) How is this possible?
3. What three kinds of love should be cultivated by marriage mates?

Mutual love and respect lead to success in marriage

that one can have for a member of the opposite sex. (Proverbs 5:15-20) Of course, all of these should be cultivated by a husband and a wife. But there is a fourth kind of love, more important than the others.

⁴ In the original language of the Christian Greek Scriptures, the word for this fourth kind of love is *a·ga′pe*. That word is used at 1 John 4:8, where we are told: "God is love." Indeed, "we love, because [God] first loved us." (1 John 4:19) A Christian cultivates such love first for Jehovah God and then for fellow humans. (Mark 12:29-31) The word *a·ga′pe* is also used at Ephesians 5:2, which states: "Go on

---

4. What is a fourth kind of love?

walking in love, just as the Christ also loved you and delivered himself up for you." Jesus said that this kind of love would identify his true followers: "By this all will know that you are my disciples, if you have love [a·ga'pe] among yourselves." (John 13:35) Notice, too, the use of a·ga'pe at 1 Corinthians 13: 13: "There remain faith, hope, love, these three; but the greatest of these is love [a·ga'pe]."

⁵ What makes this a·ga'pe love greater than faith and hope? It is governed by principles—right principles—found in God's Word. (Psalm 119:105) It is an unselfish concern for doing to others what is right and good from God's standpoint, whether the recipient appears to deserve it or not. Such love enables marriage partners to follow the Bible's counsel: "Continue putting up with one another and forgiving one another freely if anyone has a cause for complaint against another. Even as Jehovah freely forgave you, so do you also." (Colossians 3:13) Loving married couples have and cultivate "intense love [a·ga'pe] for [each other], because love covers a multitude of sins." (1 Peter 4:8) Notice that love covers mistakes. It does not eliminate them, since no imperfect human can be free from error.—Psalm 130: 3, 4; James 3:2.

⁶ When such love of God and of each other is cultivated by a married couple, their marriage will last and be happy, for "love never fails." (1 Corinthians 13:8) Love is "a perfect bond of union." (Colossians 3:14) If you are married, how can you and your mate cultivate this kind of love? Read God's Word together, and talk about it. Study Jesus' example of love and try to imitate him, to think and act like

5, 6. (a) Why is love greater than faith and hope? (b) What are some reasons why love will help make a marriage last?

him. In addition, attend Christian meetings, where God's Word is taught. And pray for God's help to develop this elevated kind of love, which is a fruit of God's holy spirit.—Proverbs 3:5, 6; John 17:3; Galatians 5:22; Hebrews 10:24, 25.

THE SECOND KEY

7 If two married people really love each other, then they will also have respect for each other, and respect is the second key to a happy marriage. Respect is defined as "giving consideration to others, honoring them." God's Word counsels all Christians, including husbands and wives: "In showing honor to one another take the lead." (Romans 12:10) The apostle Peter wrote: "You husbands, continue dwelling in like manner with [your wives] according to knowledge, assigning them honor as to a weaker vessel, the feminine one." (1 Peter 3:7) The wife is counseled to "have deep respect for her husband." (Ephesians 5:33) If you want to honor someone, you are kind to that person, respectful of that one's dignity and expressed views, and ready to fulfill any reasonable request made of you.

8 Those who wish to enjoy a happy marriage show respect for their mates by "keeping an eye, not in personal interest upon just [their] own matters, but also in personal interest upon those of [their] mates]." (Philippians 2:4) They do not consider what is good only for themselves—which would be selfish. Instead, they consider what is best also for their mates. Indeed, they give that the priority.

9 Respect will help marriage partners to acknowl-

---

7. What is respect, and who should show respect in marriage?
8-10. What are some ways that respect will help to make a marriage union stable and happy?

edge differences in viewpoint. It is not reasonable to expect two people to have identical views on everything. What may be important to a husband may not be as important to a wife, and what a wife likes may not be what a husband likes. But each should respect the views and choices of the other, as long as these are within the boundaries of Jehovah's laws and principles. (1 Peter 2:16; compare Philemon 14.) Further, each should respect the dignity of the other by not making that one the object of demeaning comments or jokes, whether in public or in private.

[10] Yes, love of God and of each other and mutual respect are two vital keys to a successful marriage. How can they be applied in some of the more important areas of married life?

CHRISTLIKE HEADSHIP

[11] The Bible tells us that the man was created with attributes that would make him a successful family head. As such, the man would be responsible before Jehovah for the spiritual and physical well-being of his wife and children. He would have to make balanced decisions that reflect Jehovah's will and be a good example of godly conduct. "Let wives be in subjection to their husbands as to the Lord, because a husband is head of his wife as the Christ also is head of the congregation." (Ephesians 5:22, 23) However, the Bible says that the husband also has a head, One with authority over him. The apostle Paul wrote: "I want you to know that the head of every man is the Christ; in turn the head of a woman is the man; in turn the head of

---

11. Scripturally, who is the head in a marriage?

the Christ is God." (1 Corinthians 11:3) The wise husband learns how to exercise headship by imitating his own head, Christ Jesus.

[12] Jesus too has a head, Jehovah, and he is properly subject to Him. Jesus said: "I seek, not my own will, but the will of him that sent me." (John 5:30) What an excellent example! Jesus is "the firstborn of all creation." (Colossians 1:15) He became the Messiah. He was to be the Head of the congregation of anointed Christians and the chosen King of God's Kingdom, above all the angels. (Philippians 2:9-11; Hebrews 1:4) Despite such a lofty position and such elevated prospects, the man Jesus was not harsh, unyielding, or overly demanding. He was not a despot, constantly reminding his disciples that they had to obey him. Jesus was loving and compassionate, especially toward the downtrodden. He said: "Come to me, all you who are toiling and loaded down, and I will refresh you. Take my yoke upon you and learn from me, for I am mild-tempered and lowly in heart, and you will find refreshment for your souls. For my yoke is kindly and my load is light." (Matthew 11:28-30) It was a delight to be in his company.

[13] The husband desiring a happy family life does well to consider Jesus' fine traits. A good husband is not harsh and dictatorial, wrongly using his headship as a club to browbeat his wife. Rather, he loves and honors her. If Jesus was "lowly in heart," the husband has even more reason to be so because, unlike Jesus, he makes mistakes. When he does, he

---

12. What fine example did Jesus set both of showing subjection and of exercising headship?
13, 14. How will a loving husband exercise his headship, in imitation of Jesus?

wants his wife's understanding. Therefore, the humble husband admits his mistakes, even though the words, "I'm sorry; you were right," might be difficult to say. A wife will find it much easier to respect the headship of a modest and humble husband than that of a proud and stubborn one. In turn, the respectful wife also apologizes when she is in error.

[14] God created the woman with fine attributes that she can use in contributing to a happy marriage. A wise husband will recognize this and will not stifle her. Many women tend to have greater compassion and sensitivity, qualities that are needed in caring for a family and in nurturing human relationships. Usually, the woman is quite adept at making the home a pleasant place in which to live. The "capable wife" described in Proverbs chapter 31 had many wonderful qualities and excellent talents, and her family benefited fully from them. Why? Because the heart of her husband "has put trust" in her.—Proverbs 31:10, 11.

[15] In some cultures, a husband's authority is overemphasized, so that even to ask him a question is considered disrespectful. He may treat his wife almost like a slave. Such a wrong exercise of headship results in a poor relationship not only with his wife but also with God. (Compare 1 John 4:20, 21.) On the other hand, some husbands neglect to take the lead, letting their wives dominate the household. The husband who is properly subject to Christ does not exploit his wife or rob her of dignity. Instead, he imitates the self-sacrificing love of Jesus and does as Paul counseled: "Husbands, continue loving your wives, just as the Christ also loved the congregation

---

15. How can a husband show Christlike love and respect for his wife?

and delivered up himself for it." (Ephesians 5:25) Christ Jesus loved his followers so much that he died for them. A good husband will try to imitate that unselfish attitude, seeking the good of his wife, rather than be demanding of her. When a husband is subject to Christ and displays Christlike love and respect, his wife will be motivated to subject herself to him.—Ephesians 5:28, 29, 33.

WIFELY SUBJECTION

¹⁶ Some time after Adam was created, "Jehovah God went on to say: 'It is not good for the man to continue by himself. I am going to make a helper for him, as a complement of him.'" (Genesis 2:18) God created Eve as "a complement," not as a competitor. Marriage was not to be like a ship with two competing captains. The husband was to exercise loving headship, and the wife was to manifest love, respect, and willing submission.

¹⁷ However, a good wife is more than just submissive. She tries to be a real helper, being supportive of her husband in the decisions he makes. Of course, that is easier for her when she agrees with his decisions. But even when she does not, her active support can help his decision to have a more successful outcome.

¹⁸ A wife can help her husband to be a good head in other ways. She can express appreciation for his efforts in taking the lead, instead of criticizing him or making him feel that he can never satisfy her.

---

16. What qualities should a wife display in her relationship with her husband?

17, 18. What are some ways that a wife can be a real helper to her husband?

In dealing with her husband in a positive way, she should remember that a "quiet and mild spirit . . . is of great value in the eyes of God," not just in the eyes of her husband. (1 Peter 3:3, 4; Colossians 3:12) What if the husband is not a believer? Whether he is or not, the Scriptures encourage wives "to love their husbands, to love their children, to be sound in mind, chaste, workers at home, good, subjecting themselves to their own husbands, so that the word of God may not be spoken of abusively." (Titus 2:4, 5) If matters of conscience come up, an unbelieving husband is more likely to respect his wife's position if it is presented with a "mild temper and deep respect." Some unbelieving husbands have been "won without a word through the conduct of their wives, because of having been eyewitnesses of [their] chaste conduct together with deep respect."—1 Peter 3:1, 2, 15; 1 Corinthians 7:13-16.

[19] What if a husband asks his wife to do something forbidden by God? If that happens, she must remember that God is her primary Ruler. She takes as an example what the apostles did when they were asked by authorities to violate God's law. Acts 5:29 relates: "Peter and the other apostles said: 'We must obey God as ruler rather than men.'"

GOOD COMMUNICATION

[20] Love and respect are essential in another area of marriage—communication. The loving husband will converse with his wife about her activities, her problems, her views on various matters. She needs this. A husband who takes the time to speak

---

19. What if a husband asks his wife to break God's law?
20. What is a vital area in which love and respect are essential?

with his wife and really listens to what she says demonstrates his love and respect for her. (James 1:19) Some wives complain that their husbands spend very little time conversing with them. That is sad. True, in these busy times, husbands may work long hours outside the home, and economic circumstances may result in some wives holding a job also. But a married couple need to reserve time for each other. Otherwise, they may become independent of each other. It could lead to serious problems if they felt compelled to seek sympathetic companionship outside the marriage arrangement.

[21] The way wives and husbands communicate is important. "Pleasant sayings are . . . sweet to the soul and a healing to the bones." (Proverbs 16:24) Whether a mate is a believer or not, the Bible counsel applies: "Let your utterance be always with graciousness, seasoned with salt," that is, in good taste. (Colossians 4:6) When one has had a difficult day, a few kind, sympathetic words from one's mate can do much good. "As apples of gold in silver carvings is a word spoken at the right time for it." (Proverbs 25:11) The tone of voice and the choice of words are very important. For example, in an irritated, demanding manner, one may tell the other: "Shut that door!" But how much more "seasoned with salt" are the words, said in a calm, understanding voice, "Would you mind closing the door, please?"

[22] Good communication flourishes when there are gently spoken words, gracious looks and gestures, kindness, understanding, and tenderness. By working hard to maintain good communication,

21. How will proper speech help to keep a marriage happy?
22. What attitudes do couples need in order to maintain good communication?

both husband and wife will feel free to make their needs known, and they can be sources of comfort and help to each other in times of disappointment or stress. "Speak consolingly to the depressed souls," urges God's Word. (1 Thessalonians 5:14) There will be times when the husband is downhearted and times when the wife is. They can "speak consolingly," building each other up.—Romans 15:2.

[23] Marriage partners manifesting love and respect will not see every disagreement as a challenge. They will work hard not to be "bitterly angry" with each other. (Colossians 3:19) Both should remember that "an answer, when mild, turns away rage." (Proverbs 15:1) Be careful not to belittle or condemn a mate who pours out heartfelt feelings. Instead, view such expressions as an opportunity to gain insight into the other's viewpoint. Together, try to work out differences and come to a harmonious conclusion.

[24] Recall the occasion when Sarah recommended to her husband, Abraham, a solution to a certain problem and it did not coincide with his feelings. Yet, God told Abraham: "Listen to her voice." (Genesis 21:9-12) Abraham did, and he was blessed. Similarly, if a wife suggests something different from what her husband has in mind, he should at least listen. At the same time, a wife should not dominate the conversation but should listen to what her husband has to say. (Proverbs 25:24) For either the husband or the wife to insist on his or her own way all the time is unloving and disrespectful.

[25] Good communication is also important in a

23, 24. How will love and respect help when there are disagreements? Give an example.
25. How will good communication contribute to happiness in the intimate aspects of married life?

couple's sexual relationship. Selfishness and a lack of self-control can seriously damage this most intimate relationship in marriage. Open communication, along with patience, is essential. When each unselfishly seeks the well-being of the other, sex is rarely a serious problem. In this as in other matters, "let each one keep seeking, not his own advantage, but that of the other person."—1 Corinthians 7:3-5; 10:24.

[26] What fine counsel God's Word offers! True, every marriage will have its ups and downs. But when spouses submit to Jehovah's thinking, as revealed in the Bible, and base their relationship on principled love and respect, they can be confident that their marriage will be lasting and happy. They thus will honor not only each other but also the Originator of marriage, Jehovah God.

26. Even though every marriage will have its ups and downs, how will listening to God's Word help married couples to find happiness?

HOW CAN THESE BIBLE PRINCIPLES HELP...
A COUPLE TO ENJOY
A LASTING, HAPPY MARRIAGE?

True Christians love one another.
—John 13:35.

Christians are ready to forgive one another.
—Colossians 3:13.

There is a proper order of headship.
—1 Corinthians 11:3.

It is important to say the right thing
in the right way.—Proverbs 25:11.

CHAPTER FOUR

How Can You Manage a Household?

"THE scene of this world is changing." (1 Corinthians 7:31) Those words were written over 1,900 years ago, and how true they are today! Things *are* changing, especially with regard to family life. What was viewed as normal or traditional 40 or 50 years ago is often not acceptable today. Because of this, successfully managing a household can present enormous challenges. Nevertheless, if Scriptural counsel is heeded, you can meet those challenges.

LIVE WITHIN YOUR MEANS

2 Today many people are no longer satisfied with a simple, family-oriented life. As the commercial world produces more and more products and uses its advertising skills to try to entice the public, millions of fathers and mothers spend long hours at work so that they can buy these products. Other millions face a day-to-day struggle just to put some food on the table. They have to spend far more time at work than used to be the case, perhaps holding down two jobs, simply to pay for necessities. Yet others would be happy to find a job, since unemployment is a widespread problem. Yes, life is not always easy for the modern family, but Bible principles can help families to make the best of the situation.

1. Why can managing a household be so difficult today?
2. What economic circumstances cause stress in a family?

³ The apostle Paul experienced economic pressures. In handling them, he learned a valuable lesson, which he explains in his letter to his friend Timothy. Paul writes: "We have brought nothing into the world, and neither can we carry anything out. So, having sustenance and covering, we shall be content with these things." (1 Timothy 6:7, 8) True, a family needs more than just food and clothing. It also needs somewhere to live. The children need an education. And there are medical bills and other expenses. Still, the principle of Paul's words applies. If we are content to satisfy our *needs* rather than indulge our *wants,* life will be easier.

⁴ Another helpful principle is found in one of Jesus' illustrations. He said: "Who of you that wants to build a tower does not first sit down and calculate the expense, to see if he has enough to complete it?" (Luke 14:28) Jesus is here speaking of forethought, planning ahead. We saw in a previous chapter how this helps when a young couple are thinking of getting married. And after the marriage, it is also helpful in managing a household. Forethought in this area involves having a budget, planning in advance to make the wisest use of available resources. In this way a family can control expenses, setting money aside for spending on essentials each day or each week, and not live beyond its means.

⁵ In some countries, such budgeting might mean having to resist the urge to borrow at high inter-

---

3. What principle did the apostle Paul explain, and how can applying it help one to be successful in managing a household?
4, 5. How can forethought and planning help in household management?

est for unnecessary purchases. In others, it might mean keeping a tight rein on the use of credit cards. (Proverbs 22:7) It might also mean resisting impulse buying—purchasing something on the spur of the moment without weighing needs and consequences. Further, a budget will make it apparent that selfishly wasting money on gambling, smoking tobacco, and excessive drinking harms the family's economic situation, as well as goes contrary to Bible principles.—Proverbs 23:20, 21, 29-35; Romans 6:19; Ephesians 5:3-5.

⁶ What, though, of those who are forced to live in poverty? For one thing, they can be comforted to know that this worldwide problem is only temporary. In the rapidly approaching new world, Jehovah will eliminate poverty along with all other evils that cause misery to mankind. (Psalm 72: 1, 12-16) In the meantime, true Christians, even if they are very poor, do not feel total desperation, for they have faith in Jehovah's promise: "I will by no means leave you nor by any means forsake you." Hence, a believer can confidently say: "Jehovah is my helper; I will not be afraid." (Hebrews 13: 5, 6) In these difficult days, Jehovah has supported his worshipers in many ways when they live by his principles and put his Kingdom first in their lives. (Matthew 6:33) Great numbers of them can testify, saying, in the words of the apostle Paul: "In everything and in all circumstances I have learned the secret of both how to be full and how to hunger, both how to have an abundance and how to suffer

---

6. What Scriptural truths help those who have to live in poverty?

Caring for the
household is a
family project

want. For all things I have the strength by virtue
of him who imparts power to me."—Philippians 4:
12, 13.

SHARING THE LOAD

7 Toward the end of his earthly ministry, Jesus
said: "You must love your neighbor as yourself."
(Matthew 22:39) Applying this counsel in the family helps enormously in household management. After all, who are our nearest, dearest neighbors if
not those who share the family dwelling—husbands

7. What words of Jesus, if applied, will help in successful
household management?

and wives, parents and children? How can family members show love for one another?

⁸ One way is for each family member to do his fair share of household chores. Thus, children need to be taught to put things away after using them, whether these be clothes or toys. It may take time and effort to tidy the bed each morning, but it is a big help in the management of the household. Of course, some minor, temporary disarray is unavoidable, but all can work together to keep the home reasonably neat, as well as to clean up after meals. Laziness, self-indulgence, and a grudging, reluctant spirit have a negative effect on everyone. (Proverbs 26:14-16) On the other hand, a cheerful, willing spirit nourishes a happy family life. "God loves a cheerful giver."—2 Corinthians 9:7.

⁹ Consideration and love will help prevent a situation that is a serious problem in some homes. Mothers have traditionally been the mainstay of home-life. They have cared for the children, cleaned the home, done the family laundry, and purchased and cooked the food. In some lands, women have also customarily worked in the fields, sold produce in the market, or contributed in other ways to the family budget. Even where this was not the custom previously, necessity has compelled millions of married women to find employment outside the home. A wife and mother who works hard in these different areas deserves commendation. Like the "capable wife" described in the Bible, her days are well filled. "The

8. How can love be expressed within the family?
9, 10. (a) What burden often rests on the woman of the house, and how can this be lightened? (b) What balanced view of housework is suggested?

bread of laziness she does not eat." (Proverbs 31: 10, 27) This does not mean, though, that a woman is the only one who can work in the home. After a husband and a wife have both worked all day outside the home, should the wife alone bear the burden of work in the house while the husband and the rest of the family relax? Surely not. (Compare 2 Corinthians 8:13, 14.) So, for example, if the mother is going to get a meal ready, she may be grateful if other family members help with the preparation by setting the table, doing some of the shopping, or cleaning up a little around the house. Yes, all can share the responsibility.—Compare Galatians 6:2.

¹⁰ Some may say: "Where I live it is not the role of a man to do such things." That may be true, but would it not be good to give this matter some consideration? When Jehovah God originated the family, he did not mandate that certain work would be done only by women. On one occasion, when the faithful man Abraham was visited by special messengers from Jehovah, he personally shared in the preparation and serving of a meal for the visitors. (Genesis 18:1-8) The Bible counsels: "Husbands ought to be loving their wives as their own bodies." (Ephesians 5:28) If, at the end of the day, the husband is tired and wants to rest, is it not likely that the wife feels the same way, perhaps more so? (1 Peter 3:7) Then, would it not be appropriate and loving for the husband to help out at home?—Philippians 2:3, 4.

¹¹ Jesus is the best example of one who pleased God and brought happiness to his associates. Al-

---

11. In what way did Jesus set a fine example for each member of the household?

though he never married, Jesus is a good example for husbands, as well as for wives and children. He said of himself: "The Son of man came, not to be ministered to, but to minister," that is, to serve others. (Matthew 20:28) How delightful are those families in which all members cultivate such an attitude!

CLEANLINESS—WHY SO IMPORTANT?

[12] Another Bible principle that can help in the management of a household is found at 2 Corinthians 7:1. There we read: "Let us cleanse ourselves of every defilement of flesh and spirit." Those who obey these inspired words are acceptable to Jehovah, who requires "worship that is clean and undefiled." (James 1:27) And their household receives associated benefits.

_____
12. What does Jehovah require of those who serve him?

[13] For example, the Bible assures us that the day will come when disease and sickness will be no more. At that time, "no resident will say: 'I am sick.'" (Isaiah 33:24; Revelation 21:4, 5) Until then, however, every family has to handle sickness from time to time. Even Paul and Timothy got sick. (Galatians 4:13; 1 Timothy 5:23) Still, medical experts say that much sickness is preventable. Wise families escape some preventable illnesses if they avoid fleshly and spiritual uncleanness. Let us consider how.—Compare Proverbs 22:3.

[14] Cleanness of spirit includes moral cleanness. As is well-known, the Bible promotes high moral standards and condemns any kind of sexual intimacy outside marriage. "Neither fornicators, . . . nor adulterers, nor men kept for unnatural purposes, nor men who lie with men . . . will inherit God's kingdom." (1 Corinthians 6:9, 10) Observing these strict standards is very important for Christians living in today's degenerate world. Doing so pleases God and also helps to protect the family from sexually transmitted diseases such as AIDS, syphilis, gonorrhea, and chlamydia.—Proverbs 7:10-23.

[15] 'Cleansing oneself of every defilement of flesh' helps to protect the family from other sicknesses. Many diseases are caused by a lack of physical cleanness. A prime example is the smoking habit. Not only does smoking befoul the lungs, the clothes,

---

13. Why is cleanliness important in household management?
14. In what way can moral cleanness protect a family from sickness?
15. Give an example of a lack of physical cleanness that can cause unnecessary illness.

Keeping things clean is cheaper than buying medicine

and the very air but it also makes people ill. Millions of people die each year because they smoked tobacco. Think of it; each year millions of people would not have fallen ill and died prematurely if they had avoided that 'defilement of the flesh'!

¹⁶ Consider another example. About 3,500 years ago, God gave the nation of Israel his Law in order to organize their worship and, to a degree, their everyday life. That Law helped to protect the nation from disease by putting in place some basic rules of hygiene. One such law had to do with the disposal of human waste, which had to be properly buried away from the camp so that the area where people lived would not be polluted. (Deuteronomy 23:12, 13) That

16, 17. (a) What law given by Jehovah protected the Israelites from certain illnesses? (b) How can the principle behind Deuteronomy 23:12, 13 be applied in all households?

ancient law is still good counsel. Even today people get sick and die because they do not follow it.*

[17] In harmony with the principle behind that Israelite law, the family's bathroom and toilet area —whether inside or outside the dwelling—should be kept clean and disinfected. If the toilet area is not kept clean and covered, flies will gather there and spread germs to other areas of the home—and onto the food we eat! Further, children and adults should wash their hands after visiting this area. Otherwise, they bring germs back with them on their skin. According to a French doctor, hand washing "is still one of the best guarantees for the prevention of certain digestive, respiratory, or skin infections."

[18] True, cleanliness is a challenge in a poor neighborhood. One who is acquainted with such localities explained: "The oppressively hot climate makes the work of cleaning doubly hard. Dust storms cover every crevice of a house with fine brown powder. . . . Burgeoning populations in cities, as well as in some rural areas, also create health hazards. Open sewers, piles of uncollected garbage, filthy communal toilets, disease-carrying rats, cockroaches, and flies have become common sights."

[19] Maintaining cleanliness under these conditions is difficult. Still, it is worth the effort. Soap and water and a little extra work are cheaper than med-

---

* In a manual advising how to avoid diarrhea—a common disease that leads to many infant deaths—the World Health Organization states: "If there is no latrine: defecate away from the house, and from areas where children play, and at least 10 metres from the water supply; cover the faeces with earth."

18, 19. What suggestions are given for maintaining a clean house even in a poor neighborhood?

icine and hospital bills. If you live in such an environment, as far as possible, keep your own house and yard clean and free of animal droppings. If the path to your home tends to get muddy during rainy periods, could you put down gravel or stones to help keep mud out of the house? If shoes or sandals are used, can these be removed before the wearer enters the home? Also, you must keep your water supply free from contamination. It is estimated that at least two million deaths a year are due to diseases associated with dirty water and poor sanitation.

[20] A clean home depends on everyone—mother, father, children, and visitors. One mother of eight children in Kenya said: "All have learned to do their part." A clean, tidy home reflects well on the whole family. A Spanish proverb states: "There is no conflict between poverty and cleanliness." Whether one lives in a mansion, an apartment, a humble home, or a shack, cleanliness is a key to a healthier family.

ENCOURAGEMENT MAKES US FLOURISH

[21] When discussing the capable wife, the book of Proverbs says: "Her sons have risen up and proceeded to pronounce her happy; her owner rises up, and he praises her." (Proverbs 31:28) When was the last time you commended a member of your family? Really, we are like plants in springtime that are ready to blossom when they receive some warmth and moisture. In our case, we need the warmth of commendation. It helps for a wife to know that her husband appreciates her hard work and loving care

---

20. If the house is to be clean, who must share the responsibility?
21. In harmony with Proverbs 31:28, what will help to bring happiness to a household?

and that he does not take her for granted. (Proverbs 15:23; 25:11) And it is pleasant when a wife commends her husband for his work outside and inside the home. Children too blossom when their parents praise them for their efforts at home, at school, or in the Christian congregation. And how far a little gratitude goes! What does it cost to say: "Thank you"? Very little, yet the return in family morale can be great.

[22] For many reasons, managing a household is not easy. Still, it can be done with success. A Bible proverb says: "By wisdom a household will be built up, and by discernment it will prove firmly established." (Proverbs 24:3) Wisdom and discernment can be gained if all in the family strive to learn God's will and to apply it in their lives. A happy family is surely worth the effort!

---

22. What is needed for a household to be "firmly established," and how can this be obtained?

HOW CAN THESE BIBLE PRINCIPLES HELP . . .
A FAMILY TO MANAGE THEIR HOUSEHOLD?

It is wise to be satisfied with the necessities of life.—1 Timothy 6:7, 8.

Jehovah will not forsake those who serve him. —Hebrews 13:5, 6.

Love for others is an outstanding Christian quality.—Matthew 22:39.

Christians keep clean in body and spirit. —2 Corinthians 7:1.

CHAPTER FIVE

Train Your Child From Infancy

"**S**ONS are an inheritance from Jehovah," exclaimed an appreciative parent some 3,000 years ago. (Psalm 127:3) Indeed, the joy of parenthood is a precious reward from God, one that is available to most married people. However, those who have children soon realize that along with the joy, parenthood brings responsibilities.

² Especially today, rearing children is a formidable task. Nevertheless, many have done it with success, and the inspired psalmist points the way, saying: "Unless Jehovah himself builds the house, it is to no avail that its builders have worked hard on it." (Psalm 127:1) The more closely you follow Jehovah's instructions, the better parent you will become. The Bible says: "Trust in Jehovah with all your heart and do not lean upon your own understanding." (Proverbs 3:5) Are you willing to listen to Jehovah's counsel as you embark on your 20-year child-raising project?

ACCEPTING THE BIBLE'S VIEW

³ In many homes around the world, men view child training as chiefly woman's work. True, the

---

1, 2. To whom should parents look for help in raising their children?

3. What responsibility do fathers have in the raising of children?

Word of God points to the father's role as principal breadwinner. However, it also says that he has responsibilities in the home. The Bible says: "Prepare your work out of doors, and make it ready for yourself in the field. Afterward you must also build up your household." (Proverbs 24:27) In God's view, fathers and mothers are partners in child training. —Proverbs 1:8, 9.

[4] How do you view your children? Reports say that in Asia "baby girls often receive a poor welcome." Bias against girls reportedly still exists in Latin America, even among "more enlightened families." The truth is, though, girls are not second-class children. Jacob, a noted father of ancient times, described all his offspring, including any daughters born up to that time, as "the children with whom God has favored [me]." (Genesis 33:1-5; 37:35) Likewise, Jesus blessed all "the young children" (boys and girls) that were brought to him. (Matthew 19:13-15) We can be sure that he reflected Jehovah's view.—Deuteronomy 16:14.

[5] Does your community expect a woman to give birth to as many children as possible? Rightfully, how many children a married couple have is their personal decision. What if parents lack the means to feed, clothe, and educate numerous children? Surely, the couple should consider this when deciding on the size of their family. Some couples who cannot support all their children entrust relatives with the responsibility to raise some of them. Is this

---

4. Why should we not view male children as superior to female?
5. What considerations should govern a couple's decision as to the size of their family?

practice desirable? Not really. And it does not relieve the parents of their obligation toward their children. The Bible says: "If anyone does not provide for those who are his own, and especially for those who are members of his household, he has disowned the faith." (1 Timothy 5:8) Responsible couples try to plan the size of their "household" so that they can 'provide for those who are their own.' Can they practice birth control in order to do this? That too is a personal decision, and if married couples do decide on this course, the choice of contraceptive is also a personal matter. "Each one will carry his own load." (Galatians 6:5) However, birth control that involves any form of abortion goes contrary to Bible principles. Jehovah God is "the source of life." (Psalm 36:9) Therefore, to snuff out a life after it has been conceived would show gross disrespect for Jehovah and is tantamount to murder.—Exodus 21:22, 23; Psalm 139:16; Jeremiah 1:5.

FILLING YOUR CHILD'S NEEDS

[6] Proverbs 22:6 says: "Train up a boy according to the way for him." Training children is another major parental duty. When, though, should that training start? Very early. The apostle Paul noted that Timothy had been trained "from infancy." (2 Timothy 3:15) The Greek word used here can refer to a small baby or even an unborn child. (Luke 1:41, 44; Acts 7:18-20) Hence, Timothy received training from when he was very young—and rightly so. Infancy is the ideal time to begin training a child. Even a young baby has a hunger for knowledge.

---

6. When should the training of a child begin?

7 "When I first saw my baby," says one mother, "I fell in love with him." So do most mothers. That beautiful attachment between mother and baby grows as they spend time together following the birth. Nursing adds to that intimacy. (Compare 1 Thessalonians 2:7.) A mother's caressing her baby and talking to it are crucial to filling the baby's emotional needs. (Compare Isaiah 66:12.) But what about the father? He too should form a close connection with his new offspring. Jehovah himself is an example of this. In the book of Proverbs, we learn of Jehovah's relationship with his only-begotten Son, who is represented as saying: "Jehovah himself produced me as the beginning of his way . . . I came to be the one he was specially fond of day by day." (Proverbs 8:22, 30; John 1:14) Similarly, a good father cultivates a warm, loving relationship with his child right from the beginning of the child's life. "Show lots of affection," says one parent. "No child ever died from hugs and kisses."

8 But babies need more. From the moment of birth, their brains are ready to receive and store information, and parents are a primary source of this. Take language as an example. Researchers say that how well a child learns to talk and to read is "thought to be closely related to the nature of the child's early interaction with his parents." Talk and read to your child from babyhood on. Soon he will want to copy you, and before long you will be teach-

7. (a) Why is it important that both parents develop a close relationship with a baby? (b) What relationship existed between Jehovah and his only-begotten Son?
8. What mental stimulation should parents give babies as soon as possible?

ing him to read. Likely, he will be able to read before entering school. That will be especially helpful if you live in a country where teachers are few and classrooms are crowded.

⁹ The foremost concern of Christian parents is filling their child's spiritual needs. (See Deuteronomy 8:3.) With what goal? To help their child to develop a Christlike personality, in effect, to put on "the new personality." (Ephesians 4:24) For this they need to consider proper building materials and proper building methods.

INCULCATE THE TRUTH IN YOUR CHILD

¹⁰ The quality of a building depends largely on the sort of materials used in the structure. The apostle Paul said that the best construction materials for Christian personalities are "gold, silver, precious stones." (1 Corinthians 3:10-12) These represent qualities such as faith, wisdom, discernment, loyalty, respect, and loving appreciation for Jehovah and his laws. (Psalm 19:7-11; Proverbs 2:1-6; 3:13, 14) How can parents help their children from earliest childhood to develop these qualities? By following a procedure outlined long ago.

¹¹ Shortly before the nation of Israel entered the Promised Land, Jehovah told Israelite parents: "These words that I am commanding you today must prove to be on your heart; and you must inculcate them in your son and speak of them when

---

9. What is the most important goal that parents need to remember?
10. What qualities do children need to develop?
11. How did Israelite parents help their children to develop godly personalities?

you sit in your house and when you walk on the road and when you lie down and when you get up." (Deuteronomy 6:6, 7) Yes, parents need to be examples, companions, communicators, and teachers.

¹² *Be an example.* First, Jehovah said: "These words . . . must prove to be on your heart." Then, he added: "You must inculcate them in your son." So godly qualities must first be in the parent's heart. The parent must love the truth and live it. Only then can he reach the child's heart. (Proverbs 20:7) Why? Because children are influenced more by what they see than by what they hear.—Luke 6:40; 1 Corinthians 11:1.

¹³ *Be a companion.* Jehovah told parents in Israel: 'Speak with your children when you sit in your house and when you walk on the road.' This requires spending time with the children no matter how busy the parents are. Jesus evidently felt that children were deserving of his time. During the final days of his ministry, "people began bringing him young children for him to touch these." What was Jesus' reaction? "He took the children into his arms and began blessing them." (Mark 10:13, 16) Imagine, the final hours of Jesus' life were ticking away. Still, he gave these children his time and attention. What a fine lesson!

¹⁴ *Be a communicator.* Spending time with your child will help you to communicate with him. The more you communicate, the better you will dis-

---

12. Why is it vital that parents be good examples?
13. In giving attention to their children, how can Christian parents copy Jesus' example?
14. Why is it beneficial for parents to spend time with their child?

Parents, be examples, companions, communicators, and teachers

cern how his personality is developing. Remember, though, communicating is more than talking. "I had to develop the art of listening," said a mother in Brazil, "listening with my heart." Her patience bore fruit when her son began to share his feelings with her.

¹⁵ Children need "a time to laugh . . . and a time to skip about," a time for recreation. (Ecclesiastes 3:1, 4; Zechariah 8:5) Recreation is very productive when parents and children enjoy it together. It is a sad fact that in many homes recreation means watching television. While some television

15. What needs to be kept in mind when it comes to recreation?

programs may be entertaining, many destroy good values, and watching television tends to stifle communication in a family. Therefore, why not do something creative with your children? Sing, play games, associate with friends, visit enjoyable places. Such activities encourage communication.

[16] *Be a teacher.* "You must inculcate [these words] in your son," said Jehovah. The context tells you *what* and *how* to teach. First, "you must love Jehovah your God with all your heart and all your soul and all your vital force." (Deuteronomy 6:5) Then, "*these words* . . . you must inculcate." Impart instruction aimed at developing whole-souled love for Jehovah and his laws. (Compare Hebrews 8:10.) The word "inculcate" means to teach by repetition. So Jehovah, in effect, tells you that the primary way to help your children develop a godly personality is to talk about him on a consistent basis. This includes having a *regular* Bible study with them.

[17] Most parents know that getting information into a child's heart is not easy. The apostle Peter urged fellow Christians: "As newborn infants, form a longing for the unadulterated milk belonging to the word." (1 Peter 2:2) The expression "*form* a longing" suggests that many do not naturally hunger for spiritual food. Parents may need to find ways to develop that longing in their child.

[18] Jesus reached hearts by using illustrations. (Mark 13:34; Luke 10:29-37) This teaching method is

---

16. What should parents teach their children about Jehovah, and how should they do so?
17. What may parents need to develop in their child? Why?
18. What are some teaching methods of Jesus that parents are encouraged to imitate?

especially effective with children. Teach Bible principles by using colorful, interesting stories, perhaps those found in the publication *My Book of Bible Stories*.* Get the children involved. Let them use their creativity in drawing and acting out Bible events. Jesus also used questions. (Matthew 17:24-27) Imitate his method during your family study. Instead of simply stating a law of God, ask questions like, Why did Jehovah give us this law? What will happen if we keep it? What will happen if we do not keep it? Such questions help a child to reason and to see that God's laws are practical and good.—Deuteronomy 10:13.

¹⁹ By being an example, a companion, a communicator, and a teacher, you can help your child from his earliest years to form a close personal relationship with Jehovah God. This relationship will encourage your child to be happy as a Christian. He will strive to live up to his faith even when faced with peer pressure and temptations. Always help him to appreciate this precious relationship.—Proverbs 27:11.

THE VITAL NEED OF DISCIPLINE

²⁰ Discipline is training that corrects the mind and heart. Children need it constantly. Paul counsels fathers to "go on bringing [their children] up in the discipline and mental-regulating of Jehovah." (Ephesians 6:4) Parents should discipline in love,

---

* Published by the Watchtower Bible and Tract Society of New York, Inc.

19. If parents follow Bible principles in dealing with their children, what great advantages will the children enjoy?
20. What is discipline, and how should it be applied?

just as Jehovah does. (Hebrews 12:4-11) Discipline based on love can be conveyed by reasoning. Hence, we are told to "listen to discipline." (Proverbs 8:33) How should discipline be given?

²¹ Some parents think that disciplining their children involves merely speaking to them in threatening tones, scolding them, or even insulting them. However, on the same subject, Paul cautions: "You, fathers, do not be irritating your children." (Ephesians 6:4) All Christians are urged to be "gentle toward all . . . instructing with mildness those not favorably disposed." (2 Timothy 2:24, 25) Christian parents, while recognizing the need for firmness, try to keep these words in mind when disciplining their children. At times, though, reasoning is insufficient, and some kind of punishment may be needed.—Proverbs 22:15.

²² Different children require different kinds of discipline. Some are not "corrected by mere words." For them, the occasional punishment administered for disobedience may be lifesaving. (Proverbs 17:10; 23: 13, 14; 29:19) A child, though, should understand why he is being punished. "The rod *and* reproof are what give wisdom." (Proverbs 29:15; Job 6:24) Moreover, punishment has boundaries. "I shall have to chastise you *to the proper degree*," said Jehovah to his people. (Jeremiah 46:28b) The Bible in no way endorses angry whippings or severe beatings, which bruise and even injure a child.—Proverbs 16:32.

---

21. What principles should parents bear in mind when disciplining their children?
22. If a child needs to be punished, what must he be helped to understand?

EFFECTIVE DISCIPLINE

One meaningful form of discipline is to make children feel the unpleasant consequences of wrong behavior. (Galatians 6:7; compare Exodus 34:6, 7.) If, for instance, your child makes a mess, cleaning it up by himself may make the strongest impression. Has he treated someone unfairly? Requiring that he apologize may correct this wrong trend. Another form of discipline is the denial of privileges for a time in order to drive home the needed lesson. In this way the child learns the wisdom of sticking to right principles.

²³ When Jehovah warned his people that he would discipline them, he first said: "Do not be afraid . . . for I am with you." (Jeremiah 46:28a) Likewise, parental discipline, in whatever appropriate form, should never leave a child feeling rejected. (Colossians 3:21) Rather, the child should sense that discipline is given because the parent is 'with him,' on his side.

PROTECT YOUR CHILD FROM HARM

²⁴ Many adults look back on their childhood as a happy time. They recall a warm feeling of safety, a certainty that their parents would look after them no matter what. Parents want their children to feel that way, but in today's degenerate world, it is harder than it used to be to keep children safe.

---

23. What should a child be able to discern when he is punished by his parents?
24, 25. What is one ugly threat from which children need protection these days?

[25] One ugly threat that has grown in recent years is sexual molestation of children. In Malaysia, reports of child molestation quadrupled over a period of ten years. In Germany some 300,000 children are sexually abused each year, while in a South American country, according to one study, the estimated annual number is a staggering 9,000,000! Tragically, the majority of these children are molested in their own home by people they know and trust. But children should have a strong defense in their parents. How can parents be protectors?

[26] Since experience shows that children who know little about sex are especially vulnerable to child molesters, a major preventive step is to educate the child, even when he is still young. Knowledge can provide protection "from the bad way, from the man speaking perverse things." (Proverbs 2: 10-12) What knowledge? Knowledge of Bible principles, of what is morally right and wrong. Knowledge too that some grown-ups do bad things and that a young person does not have to obey when people suggest inappropriate acts. (Compare Daniel 1:4, 8; 3:16-18.) Do not limit such instruction to a onetime talk. Most young children need to have a lesson repeated before they remember it well. As children grow a little older, a father would lovingly respect his daughter's right to privacy, and a mother her son's—thus reinforcing a child's sense of what is proper. And, of course, one of the best safeguards against abuse is close supervision by you as parents.

---

26. What are some ways that children can be kept safe, and how can knowledge protect a child?

FAMILY HAPPINESS

SEEK DIVINE GUIDANCE

²⁷ Truly, the training of a child from infancy is a challenge, but believing parents do not have to face the challenge alone. Back in the days of the Judges, when a man named Manoah learned that he was going to be a father, he asked Jehovah for guidance on raising his child. Jehovah answered his prayers. —Judges 13:8, 12, 24.

²⁸ In a similar way today, as believing parents raise their children, they can also speak to Jehovah in prayer. Being a parent is hard work, but there are great rewards. A Christian couple in Hawaii says: "You have 12 years to get your work done before those critical teen years. But if you have worked hard to apply Bible principles, it is time to reap joy and peace when they decide they want to serve Jehovah from the heart." (Proverbs 23:15, 16) When your child makes that decision, you too will be moved to exclaim: "Sons [and daughters] are an inheritance from Jehovah."

27, 28. Who is the parents' greatest Source of help when they face the challenge of raising a child?

> #### HOW CAN THESE BIBLE PRINCIPLES HELP . . .
> #### PARENTS TO TRAIN THEIR CHILDREN?
> ---
>
> Trust in Jehovah.—Proverbs 3:5.
>
> Be responsible.—1 Timothy 5:8.
>
> Jehovah is a loving Father.—Proverbs 8:22, 30.
>
> Parents are responsible for instructing their children.—Deuteronomy 6:6, 7.
>
> Discipline is needed.—Ephesians 6:4.

CHAPTER SIX

Help Your Teenager to Thrive

Having a teenager in the house is very different from having a five-year-old or even a ten-year-old. The teen years bring their own challenges and problems, but they can also bring joys and rewards. Examples such as Joseph, David, Josiah, and Timothy show that young people can act responsibly and have a fine relationship with Jehovah. (Genesis 37:2-11; 1 Samuel 16:11-13; 2 Kings 22:3-7; Acts 16:1, 2) Many teenagers today prove the same point. Likely, you know some of them.

² Yet, for some the teen years are turbulent. Adolescents experience emotional ups and downs. Teenage boys and girls may want to be more independent, and they may resent limits placed on them by their parents. Yet, such youths are still quite inexperienced and in need of loving, patient help from their parents. Yes, the teen years can be exciting, but they can also be confusing—both for parents and for teenagers. How can youths be helped during these years?

³ Parents who follow Bible counsel give their adolescent offspring the best possible opportunity to make their way successfully through those trials to responsible adulthood. In all lands and during all

_____
1, 2. What challenges and what joys can the teen years bring?
3. In what way can parents give their adolescent offspring a fine opportunity in life?

64   FAMILY HAPPINESS

time periods, parents and teenagers who applied Bible principles together have been blessed with success.—Psalm 119:1.

HONEST AND OPEN COMMUNICATION

⁴ The Bible says: "There is a frustrating of plans where there is no confidential talk." (Proverbs 15: 22) If confidential talk was necessary when the children were younger, it is especially vital during the teen years—when youngsters likely spend less time at home and more time with school friends or other companions. If there is no confidential talk —no honest and open communication between children and parents—teenagers can become strangers in the house. So how can the lines of communication be kept open?

⁵ Both teenagers and parents must play their part in this. True, adolescents may find it more difficult to talk with their parents than they did when they were younger. Nevertheless, remember that "when there is no skillful direction, the people fall; but there is salvation in the multitude of counselors." (Proverbs 11:14) These words apply to all, young and old alike. Teenagers who realize this will understand that they still need skillful direction, since they are facing more-complex issues than before. They should recognize that their believing parents are well qualified as counselors because they are more experienced in life and have proved their loving concern over many years. Hence, at this stage

---

4. Why is confidential talk especially important during the teen years?
5. How are teenagers encouraged to view the matter of communicating with their parents?

in their life, wise teenagers will not turn away from their parents.

⁶ Open communication means that the parent will try hard to be available when the teenager feels the need to talk. If you are a parent, make sure that communication is open at least from your side. This may not be easy. The Bible says that there is "a time to keep quiet and a time to speak." (Ecclesiastes 3:7) When your teenager feels it is a time to speak, it may be your time to keep quiet. Perhaps you have set that time aside for personal study, relaxation, or work around the house. Still, if your youngster wants to talk to you, try to adjust your plans and listen. Otherwise, he may not try again. Remember the example of Jesus. On one occasion, he had scheduled a time to relax. But when people came crowding around to hear him, he put off resting and began to teach them. (Mark 6:30-34) Most teenagers realize that their parents lead busy lives, but they need the reassurance that their parents are there for them if needed. Hence, be available and be understanding.

⁷ Try to remember what it was like when you were a teenager, and do not lose your sense of humor! Parents need to enjoy being with their children. When there is free time available, how do the parents spend it? If they always want to use their free time doing things that do not include their family, their teenagers will be quick to notice. If adolescents come to the conclusion that school friends think more of them than their parents do,

---

6. What attitude will wise and loving parents have as to communicating with their teenagers?
7. What do parents need to avoid?

they are bound to have problems.

WHAT TO COMMUNICATE

[8] If parents have not already inculcated in their children an appreciation for honesty and hard work, they should by all means do so during the teen years. (1 Thessalonians 4:11; 2 Thessalonians 3:10) It is also vital for them to make sure that their children wholeheartedly believe in the importance of living a moral

Be available when your teenager needs to talk

and clean life. (Proverbs 20:11) A parent communicates much in these areas by way of example. Just as unbelieving husbands can be "won without a word through the conduct of their wives," so teenagers can learn right principles through the conduct of their parents. (1 Peter 3:1) Still, example on its own is never enough, since children are also exposed to many bad examples and to a flood of enticing propaganda outside the home. Caring parents, therefore, need to know their teenagers' views on what they see and hear, and this calls for meaningful conversation.—Proverbs 20:5.

---

8. How can appreciation for honesty, hard work, and proper conduct be impressed on children?

⁹ This is particularly true when it comes to sexual matters. Parents, are you embarrassed to discuss sex with your children? Even if you are, make the effort to do so, for your young ones will surely learn about the subject from someone. If they do not learn from you, who knows what distorted information they will get? In the Bible, Jehovah does not shy away from matters of a sexual nature, and neither should parents.—Proverbs 4:1-4; 5:1-21.

¹⁰ Thankfully, the Bible contains clear guidance in the area of sexual conduct, and the Watchtower Society has published much helpful information showing that this guidance still applies in the modern world. Why not make use of this help? For example, why not review with your son or daughter the section "Sex and Morals" in the book *Questions Young People Ask—Answers That Work*? You may be pleasantly surprised at the results.

¹¹ What is the most important subject that parents and children should discuss? The apostle Paul referred to it when he wrote: "Go on bringing [your children] up in the discipline and mental-regulating of Jehovah." (Ephesians 6:4) Children need to keep learning about Jehovah. In particular, they need to learn to love him, and they should want to serve him. Here, too, much can be taught by example. If adolescents see that their parents love God 'with their whole heart and with their whole soul and with their whole mind' and that this produces good fruits in their parents' lives, they may well be influ-

9, 10. Why should parents make sure to instruct their children about sexual matters, and how can they do this?
11. What is a most effective way for parents to teach their children how to serve Jehovah?

Regular Bible study is essential for the family

enced to do the same. (Matthew 22:37) Similarly, if young people see that their parents have a reasonable view of material things, putting God's Kingdom first, they will be helped to develop the same mental attitude.—Ecclesiastes 7:12; Matthew 6:31-33.

[12] A weekly family Bible study is an outstanding help in communicating spiritual values to young people. (Psalm 119:33, 34; Proverbs 4:20-23) Having such a study regularly is vital. (Psalm 1:1-3) Parents and their children should realize that other things must be scheduled around the family study, not vice versa. Further, the right attitude is essential if the family study is to be effective. One father said: "The secret is for the conductor to foster a relaxed yet respectful atmosphere during the family study—informal but not silly. The correct balance may not always be easy to attain, and youngsters will frequently need attitude adjustment. If

12, 13. What points should be kept in mind if the family study is to be a success?

Express love and appreciation for your children

things do not go well a time or two, persevere and look ahead to the next time." This same father said that in his prayer before each study, he specifically requested help from Jehovah for the right viewpoint on the part of all involved.—Psalm 119:66.

¹³ Conducting the family study is the responsibility of believing parents. True, some parents may not be gifted teachers, and it may be difficult for them to find ways to make the family study interesting. Nevertheless, if you love your teenagers "in deed and truth," you will desire to help them in a humble and honest way to advance spiritually. (1 John 3:18) They may complain from time to time, but likely they will sense your deep interest in their welfare.

¹⁴ The family study is not the only occasion to communicate matters that are spiritually important. Do you remember Jehovah's command to parents? He said: "You must apply these words of mine to your heart and your soul and bind them as a sign upon your hand, and they must serve as a frontlet

14. How can Deuteronomy 11:18, 19 be applied when communicating spiritual things to teenagers?

band between your eyes. You must also teach them to your sons, so as to speak of them when you sit in your house and when you walk on the road and when you lie down and when you get up." (Deuteronomy 11:18, 19; see also Deuteronomy 6:6, 7.) This does not mean that parents must constantly preach to their children. But a loving family head should always be on the lookout for opportunities to build up the spiritual outlook of his family.

DISCIPLINE AND RESPECT

15 Discipline is training that corrects, and it includes communication. Discipline carries the thought of correction more than of punishment —although punishment may come into the picture. Your children needed discipline when they were younger, and now that they are teenagers, they still need some form of it, perhaps even more so. Wise teenagers know that this is true.

16 The Bible says: "Anyone foolish disrespects the discipline of his father, but anyone regarding reproof is shrewd." (Proverbs 15:5) We learn much from this scripture. It implies that discipline will be given. A teenager cannot 'regard reproof' if it is not given. Jehovah gives the responsibility for administering discipline to the parents, particularly the father. However, the responsibility for listening to that discipline belongs to the teenager. He will learn more and make fewer mistakes if he heeds the wise discipline of his father and mother. (Proverbs 1:8) The Bible says: "The one neglecting discipline comes to poverty and dishonor, but the one

_____
15, 16. (a) What is discipline? (b) Who is responsible for administering discipline, and who has the responsibility to ensure that it will be heeded?

keeping a reproof is the one that is glorified."—Proverbs 13:18.

¹⁷ When disciplining teenagers, parents need to be balanced. They should avoid being so strict that they irritate their offspring, perhaps even damaging their children's self-confidence. (Colossians 3: 21) And yet parents do not want to be so permissive that their youngsters miss out on vital training. Such permissiveness can be disastrous. Proverbs 29:17 says: "Chastise your son and he will bring you rest and give much pleasure to your soul." However, verse 21 says: "If one is pampering one's servant from youth on, in his later life he will even become a thankless one." Although this verse is talking about a servant, it applies with equal measure to any youngster in the household.

¹⁸ In truth, proper discipline is a proof of the parent's love for his child. (Hebrews 12:6, 11) If you are a parent, you know that it is difficult to maintain consistent, reasonable discipline. For the sake of peace, it may seem easier to allow an obstinate teenager to do what he wants. In the long run, however, a parent who follows this latter course will pay for it with a household that is out of control.—Proverbs 29:15; Galatians 6:9.

WORK AND PLAY

¹⁹ In earlier times children were usually expected to help out in the home or on the farm. Today many

---

17. What balance do parents need to aim for when administering discipline?
18. Of what is discipline an evidence, and what is avoided when parents administer consistent discipline?
19, 20. How can parents deal wisely with the matter of recreation for their teenagers?

teenagers have a lot of unsupervised spare time. To fill that time, the commercial world provides a superabundance of material to fill leisure time. Add to this the fact that the world puts very little value on Bible standards of morality, and you have a formula for potential disaster.

[20] Hence, the judicious parent maintains the right to make final decisions about recreation. Do not forget, though, that the teenager is growing up. Each year, he or she will likely hope to be treated more like an adult. Thus, it is wise for a parent to allow more latitude in the choice of recreation as the teenager gets older—as long as those choices reflect progress toward spiritual maturity. At times, the teenager may make unwise choices in music, associates, and so on. When this happens, it should be discussed with the teenager so that better choices will be made in the future.

[21] How much time should be allotted for recreation? In some lands teenagers are led to believe that they are entitled to continual entertainment. Hence, an adolescent may plan his schedule so that he goes from one "good time" to the next. It is up to the parents to convey the lesson that time should also be spent on other things, such as the family, personal study, association with spiritually mature persons, Christian meetings, and household chores. This will keep the "pleasures of this life" from choking out God's Word.—Luke 8:11-15.

[22] King Solomon said: "I have come to know that

21. How will reasonableness in the amount of time spent in recreation protect a teenager?
22. With what should recreation be balanced in a teenager's life?

there is nothing better for them than to rejoice and to do good during one's life; and also that every man should eat and indeed drink and see good for all his hard work. It is the gift of God." (Ecclesiastes 3:12, 13) Yes, rejoicing is part of a balanced life. But so is hard work. Many teenagers today do not learn the satisfaction that comes from hard work or the feeling of self-respect that comes from tackling a problem and solving it. Some are not given the opportunity to develop a skill or trade with which to support themselves in later life. Here is a real challenge for the parent. Will you make sure that your young one has such opportunities? If you can succeed in teaching your teenager to value and even enjoy hard work, he or she will develop a healthy outlook that will bring a lifetime of benefits.

FROM TEENAGER TO ADULT

[23] Even when you have problems with your teenager, the scripture still holds true: "Love never fails." (1 Corinthians 13:8) Never cease to show the love that you undoubtedly feel. Ask yourself, 'Do I compliment each child on his successes in handling problems or overcoming obstacles? Do I seize opportunities to express my love and appreciation for my children, before those opportunities pass?' Although at times there may be misunderstandings, if teenagers feel assured of your love for them, they are more likely to return that love.

[24] Of course, as children grow to adulthood, they will eventually make very weighty decisions for themselves. In some cases parents may not like

---

23. How can parents encourage their teenagers?
24. What Scriptural principle holds true as a general rule in bringing up children, but what should be borne in mind?

those decisions. What if their child decides not to continue serving Jehovah God? This can occur. Even some of Jehovah's own spirit sons rejected his counsel and proved rebellious. (Genesis 6:2; Jude 6) Children are not computers, which can be programmed to act the way we want. They are creatures with free will, responsible before Jehovah for the decisions they make. Still, Proverbs 22:6 holds true as a general rule: "Train up a boy according to the way for him; even when he grows old he will not turn aside from it."

²⁵ So then, show your children plenty of love. Do your best to follow Bible principles in raising them. Set a fine example of godly conduct. Thus you will give your children the best opportunity to grow up to be responsible, God-fearing adults. This is the finest way for parents to show gratitude to Jehovah for the privilege of parenthood.

---

25. What is the finest way for parents to show gratitude to Jehovah for the privilege of parenthood?

HOW CAN THESE BIBLE PRINCIPLES HELP... PARENTS TO RAISE THEIR TEENAGERS?

Communication is needed.—Proverbs 15:22.

We should regularly consider God's Word.
—Psalm 1:1, 2.

A shrewd person listens to discipline.
—Proverbs 15:5.

Both work and play have their place.
—Ecclesiastes 3:12, 13.

CHAPTER SEVEN

Is There a Rebel in the House?

A FEW days before his death, Jesus asked a group of Jewish religious leaders a thought-provoking question. He said: "What do you think? A man had two children. Going up to the first, he said, 'Child, go work today in the vineyard.' In answer this one said, 'I will, sir,' but did not go out. Approaching the second, he said the same. In reply this one said, 'I will not.' Afterwards he felt regret and went out.

1, 2. (a) What illustration did Jesus give to highlight the unfaithfulness of Jewish religious leaders? (b) What point about adolescents can we learn from Jesus' illustration?

Which of the two did the will of his father?" The Jewish leaders replied: "The latter."—Matthew 21:28-31.

2 Jesus was here highlighting the unfaithfulness of the Jewish leaders. They were like the first son, promising to do God's will and then not keeping their promise. But many parents will recognize that Jesus' illustration was based on a good understanding of family life. As he so well showed, it is often difficult to know what young people are thinking or to predict what they will do. A young person may cause many problems during his adolescence and then grow up to be a responsible, well-respected adult. This is something to keep in mind when we discuss the problem of teenage rebellion.

WHAT IS A REBEL?

3 From time to time, you may hear of teenagers who outrightly rebel against their parents. You may even personally know of a family in which a teenager seems impossible to control. However, it is not always easy to know whether a child is really a rebel. Moreover, it can be difficult to understand why some children rebel and others—even from the same household—do not. If parents suspect that one of their children may be developing into an out-and-out rebel, what should they do? To answer this, we first have to talk about what a rebel is.

4 Simply put, a rebel is a person who willfully and consistently disobeys or resists and defies a higher authority. Of course, 'foolishness is in the heart of a child.' (Proverbs 22:15) So all children resist parental and other authority at one time or another.

---

3. Why should parents not hastily label their child a rebel?
4-6. (a) What is a rebel? (b) What should parents bear in mind if their teenager is disobedient from time to time?

This is particularly true during the time of physical and emotional development known as adolescence. A change in any person's life will create stress, and adolescence is all about change. Your teenage son or daughter is moving out of childhood and onto the road to adulthood. For this reason, during the adolescent years, some parents and children have a hard time getting along. Often parents instinctively try to put the brakes on the transition, whereas teenagers want to speed it up.

⁵ A teenager who is a rebel turns his back on parental values. Remember, though, that a few acts of disobedience do not make a rebel. And when it comes to spiritual matters, some children may at first show little or no interest in Bible truth, but they may not be rebels. As a parent, do not be quick to pin a label on your child.

⁶ Are the adolescent years of all young people characterized by rebellion against parental authority? No, not at all. Indeed, the evidence would seem to indicate that only a minority of teenagers display serious adolescent rebellion. Still, what of a child who obstinately and consistently rebels? What might provoke such rebellion?

CAUSES OF REBELLION

⁷ A major cause of rebellion is the world's satanic environment. "The whole world is lying in the power of the wicked one." (1 John 5:19) The world in Satan's power has developed a harmful culture with which Christians have to contend. (John 17:15) Much of that culture is coarser, more dangerous, and filled with more bad influences today than in

---

7. How can the satanic environment influence a child to rebel?

the past. (2 Timothy 3:1-5, 13) If parents do not educate, warn, and protect their children, young ones can easily be overwhelmed by "the spirit that now operates in the sons of disobedience." (Ephesians 2:2) Related to this is peer pressure. The Bible says: "He that is having dealings with the stupid ones will fare badly." (Proverbs 13:20) Similarly, he that keeps company with those who are imbued with the spirit of this world is likely to be influenced by that spirit. Young ones require constant help if they are to appreciate that obedience to godly principles is the foundation of the very best way of life.—Isaiah 48:17, 18.

⁸ Another cause of rebellion might be the atmosphere in the home. For example, if one parent is an alcoholic, abuses drugs, or is violent toward the other parent, the teenager's view of life can be warped. Even in relatively tranquil homes, rebellion may break out when a child feels that his parents have no interest in him. However, teenage rebellion is not always caused by external influences. Some children turn their backs on parental values despite having parents who apply godly principles and who shelter them, to a great extent, from the world around them. Why? Perhaps because of another root of our problems—human imperfection. Paul said: "Through one man [Adam] sin entered into the world and death through sin, and thus death spread to all men because they had all sinned." (Romans 5:12) Adam was a selfish rebel, and he left all his offspring a bad legacy. Some youths just choose to rebel, as their forefather did.

----

8. What factors might lead to rebellion on the part of a child?

PERMISSIVE ELI AND RESTRICTIVE REHOBOAM

[9] Something else that has led to teenage rebellion is an unbalanced view of child rearing on the part of the parents. (Colossians 3:21) Some conscientious parents severely restrict and discipline their children. Others are permissive, not providing guidelines that would protect their inexperienced adolescent. It is not always easy to strike a balance between these two extremes. And different children have different needs. One may need more oversight than another. Still, two Bible examples will help to show the dangers of being extreme in either restrictiveness or permissiveness.

[10] Ancient Israel's high priest Eli was a father. He served for 40 years, no doubt being well versed in the Law of God. Eli likely carried out his regular priestly duties quite faithfully and may even have thoroughly taught God's Law to his sons, Hophni and Phinehas. However, Eli was too indulgent with his sons. Hophni and Phinehas served as officiating priests, but they were "good-for-nothing men," interested only in satisfying their appetites and immoral desires. Yet, when they committed disgraceful acts on sacred ground, Eli did not have the courage to oust them from office. He merely gave them a feeble rebuke. By his permissiveness, Eli honored his sons more than God. As a result, his sons rebelled against Jehovah's clean worship and Eli's whole house suffered calamity.—1 Samuel 2:12-17, 22-25, 29; 3:13, 14; 4:11-22.

9. What extremes in child rearing might provoke a child to rebel?
10. Why was Eli, although likely a faithful high priest, a poor parent?

¹¹ Eli's children were already adults when these events took place, but this history underscores the danger of withholding discipline. (Compare Proverbs 29:21.) Some parents may confuse love with permissiveness, failing to set and enforce clear, consistent, and reasonable rules. They neglect to apply loving discipline, even when godly principles are violated. Because of such permissiveness, their children may end up not paying attention to parental or any other type of authority.—Compare Ecclesiastes 8:11.

¹² Rehoboam exemplifies the other extreme in handling authority. He was the last king of the united kingdom of Israel, but he was not a good king. Rehoboam had inherited a land whose people were discontented because of the burdens placed on them by his father, Solomon. Did Rehoboam show understanding? No. When a delegation asked him to remove some of the oppressive measures, he failed to heed mature advice from his older counselors and commanded that the people's yoke be made heavier. His arrogance provoked a rebellion by the ten northern tribes, and the kingdom was ripped in two.—1 Kings 12:1-21; 2 Chronicles 10:19.

¹³ Parents can learn some important lessons from the Bible account of Rehoboam. They need to "search for Jehovah" in prayer and to examine their child-rearing methods in the light of Bible principles. (Psalm 105:4) "Mere oppression may make a wise one act crazy," says Ecclesiastes 7:7.

11. What can parents learn from Eli's wrong example?
12. What mistake did Rehoboam make in the exercise of authority?
13. How can parents avoid Rehoboam's mistake?

TALK IT OUT

Adolescents will experience doubts and anxieties connected with increased independence. They may feel a little shaky about their ability to handle themselves in the world. It is as if they were trying to walk on a slippery road. You young ones, confide in your parents about your fears and the apprehensions you are experiencing. (Proverbs 23:22) Or if you feel that your parents are holding you too tightly, talk with them about your need to be granted more freedom. Plan to talk with them at a time when you are relaxed and when they are not busy. (Proverbs 15:23) Take the time really to listen to each other.

Well-thought-out boundaries give adolescents room to grow while protecting them from harm. But children should not live in an atmosphere that is so rigid and constricting that they are prevented from developing a reasonable measure of self-reliance and self-confidence. When parents strive for a balance between fair latitude and firm boundaries that are clearly marked, most teenagers will feel less inclined to rebel.

FILLING BASIC NEEDS
CAN PREVENT REBELLION

[14] Although parents rejoice to see their youngster grow physically from babyhood to adulthood, they may feel disturbed when their adolescent child begins to move from dependence to appropriate self-reliance. During this transitional period, do not be surprised if your teenager is occasionally rather

14, 15. How should parents view the development of their child?

Likely, children will grow up to be more stable if their parents help them to cope with their teenage problems

stubborn or uncooperative. Keep in mind that the goal of Christian parents should be to raise a mature, stable, and responsible Christian.—Compare 1 Corinthians 13:11; Ephesians 4:13, 14.

¹⁵ As difficult as it may be, parents need to break the habit of responding negatively to any request from their adolescent for greater independence. In a wholesome way, a child needs to grow as an individual. Indeed, at a relatively young age, some teenagers begin to develop quite a grown-up outlook. For example, the Bible says of young King Josiah: "While he was still a boy [of about 15 years], he started to search for the God of David." This outstanding teenager was clearly a responsible individual. —2 Chronicles 34:1-3.

¹⁶ However, freedom brings with it accountability. Therefore, allow your emerging adult to experience the consequences of some of his decisions and actions. The principle, "whatever a man is sowing, this he will also reap," applies to teens as well as to adults. (Galatians 6:7) Children cannot be sheltered forever. What, though, if your child wants to do something that is completely unacceptable? As a responsible parent, you have to say, "No." And, while you may explain the reasons, nothing should change your no to a yes. (Compare Matthew 5:37.) Nevertheless, try to say "No" in a calm and reasonable manner, since "an answer, when mild, turns away rage."—Proverbs 15:1.

¹⁷ Young people need the security of consistent discipline even if they do not always readily agree with the restrictions and rules. It is frustrating if rules are frequently changed, depending on the way a parent feels at the time. Further, if teenagers receive encouragement and help, as needed, in coping with diffidence, shyness, or lack of self-confidence, they will likely grow up to be more stable. Teenagers also appreciate it when they receive the trust that they have earned.—Compare Isaiah 35:3, 4; Luke 16: 10; 19:17.

¹⁸ Parents can be comforted to know that when peace, stability, and love exist within the household, the children usually flourish. (Ephesians 4: 31, 32; James 3:17, 18) Why, many youngsters have risen above even a bad home environment, com-

---

16. As children are given increased responsibility, what should they face up to?
17. What are some needs of a teenager that a parent should fill?
18. What are some encouraging truths about teenagers?

ing from families marked by alcoholism, violence, or some other harmful influence, and have grown up to be fine adults. Hence, if you provide a home where your teenagers feel secure and know that they will receive love, affection, and attention—even if that support is accompanied by reasonable restrictions and discipline in harmony with Scriptural principles—they are very likely to grow up to be adults you will be proud of.—Compare Proverbs 27:11.

WHEN CHILDREN GET INTO DIFFICULTY

[19] Good parenting certainly makes a difference. Proverbs 22:6 says: "Train up a boy according to the way for him; even when he grows old he will not turn aside from it." Still, what of children who have serious problems in spite of having good parents? Is this possible? Yes. The words of the proverb must be understood in the light of other verses that emphasize the child's responsibility to "listen" to and obey the parents. (Proverbs 1:8) Both parent and child must cooperate in applying Scriptural principles if there is to be family harmony. If parents and children do not work together, there will be difficulties.

[20] How should parents react when a teenager errs and gets into trouble? Then, especially, the youngster needs help. If the parents remember that they are dealing with an inexperienced youth, they will more easily resist the tendency to overreact. Paul counseled mature ones in the congregation: "Even though a man takes some false step before he is

19. While parents should train up a boy in the way he should go, what responsibility rests with the child?
20. When children err because of being thoughtless, what would be a wise approach by the parents?

aware of it, you who have spiritual qualifications try to readjust such a man in a spirit of mildness." (Galatians 6:1) Parents can follow this same procedure when dealing with a young person who commits an error because of being thoughtless. While clearly explaining why his conduct was wrong and how he can avoid repeating the error, the parents should make it clear that it is the wrong conduct, not the youth, that is bad.—Compare Jude 22, 23.

²¹ What if the youngster's delinquency is very serious? In that case the child needs special help and skillful direction. When a congregation member commits a serious sin, he is encouraged to repent and approach the elders for help. (James 5:14-16) Once he repents, the elders work with him to restore him spiritually. In the family the responsibility for helping the erring teenager rests with the parents, although they may need to discuss the matter with the elders. They certainly should not try to conceal from the body of elders any grave sins committed by one of their children.

²² A serious problem involving one's own children is very trying. Being distraught emotionally, parents may feel like angrily threatening the wayward offspring; but this might only embitter him. Bear in mind that the future of this young person may depend on how he is treated during this critical time. Remember, too, that Jehovah was ready to forgive when his people deviated from what was right—if they would only repent. Listen to his loving

21. Following the example of the Christian congregation, how should parents react if their children commit a serious sin?
22. In imitation of Jehovah, what attitude will parents try to maintain if their child commits a serious error?

words: "'Come, now, you people, and let us set matters straight between us,' says Jehovah. 'Though the sins of you people should prove to be as scarlet, they will be made white just like snow; though they should be red like crimson cloth, they will become even like wool.'" (Isaiah 1:18) What a fine example for parents!

23 Hence, try to encourage the wayward one to change his course. Seek sound advice from experienced parents and congregation elders. (Proverbs 11:14) Try not to act impulsively and say or do things that would make it difficult for your child to return to you. Avoid uncontrolled wrath and bitterness. (Colossians 3:8) Do not be quick to give up. (1 Corinthians 13:4, 7) While hating badness, avoid becoming hard and embittered toward your child. Most important, parents should strive to set a fine example and to keep their faith in God strong.

HANDLING A DETERMINED REBEL

24 In some cases it becomes clear that a youth has made a definite decision to rebel and completely reject Christian values. Then the focus should change to that of maintaining or rebuilding the family life of those who remain. Be careful that you do not direct all your energy to the rebel, to the neglect of the other children. Instead of trying to hide the trouble from the rest of the family, discuss the matter with them to an appropriate extent and in a reassuring way.—Compare Proverbs 20:18.

---

23. In the face of a serious sin by one of their children, how should parents act, and what should they avoid?
24. What sad situation sometimes arises in a Christian family, and how should a parent respond?

²⁵ The apostle John said of one who becomes an irreclaimable rebel in the congregation: "Never receive him into your homes or say a greeting to him." (2 John 10) Parents may feel it necessary to take a similar stand toward their own child if he is of legal age and becomes totally rebellious. As difficult and wrenching as such action may be, it is sometimes essential in order to protect the rest of the family. Your household needs your protection and continued oversight. Hence, keep on maintaining clearly defined, yet reasonable, boundaries of conduct. Communicate with the other children. Be interested in how they are doing in school and in the congregation. Also, let them know that even though you do not approve of the rebellious child's actions, you do not hate him. Condemn the bad action rather than the child. When Jacob's two sons brought ostracism upon the family because of their cruel deed, Jacob cursed their violent anger, not the sons themselves.—Genesis 34:1-31; 49:5-7.

²⁶ You may feel responsible for what has happened in your family. But if you have prayerfully done all you could, following Jehovah's counsel as well as you were able, there is no need to criticize yourself unreasonably. Take comfort in the fact that nobody can be a perfect parent, but you conscientiously tried to be a good one. (Compare Acts 20:26.) To have an out-and-out rebel in the family

---

25. (a) Following the pattern of the Christian congregation, how may parents have to proceed if a child becomes a determined rebel? (b) What should parents bear in mind if one of their children rebels?

26. From what can conscientious parents draw comfort if one of their children rebels?

is heartrending, but if it should happen to you, be assured that God understands and he will never abandon his devoted servants. (Psalm 27:10) So be determined to keep your home a safe, spiritual haven for any remaining children.

²⁷ Moreover, you should never give up hope. Your earlier efforts in proper training may eventually affect the heart of the straying child and bring him back to his senses. (Ecclesiastes 11:6) A number of Christian families have had the same experience as you, and some have seen their wayward children return, much as the father did in Jesus' parable of the prodigal son. (Luke 15:11-32) The same thing may happen to you.

---

27. Remembering the parable of the prodigal son, for what can parents of a rebellious child always hope?

HOW CAN THESE BIBLE PRINCIPLES HELP...
A PARENT TO PREVENT SERIOUS
REBELLION IN THE HOUSEHOLD?

Without help, a child can be corrupted by the world's spirit.—Proverbs 13:20; Ephesians 2:2.

Parents need to strike a balance between restrictiveness and permissiveness.
—Ecclesiastes 7:7; 8:11.

Wrong conduct must be dealt with, but in a spirit of mildness.—Galatians 6:1.

Those who commit serious sins can be "healed" if they repent and accept help.—James 5:14-16.

CHAPTER EIGHT

Protect Your Family From Destructive Influences

YOU are about to send your little boy to school, and it is pouring rain. How do you handle the situation? Do you let him go skipping out the door without any rain gear? Or do you pile on so many layers of protective clothing that he can hardly move? Of course, you do neither. You give him just what is needed to keep him dry.

[2] In a similar way, parents must find a balanced way to protect their family from the destructive influences that rain down on them from many sources —the entertainment industry, the media, peers, and at times even the schools. Some parents do little or nothing to shield their family. Others, viewing nearly all outside influences as harmful, are so restrictive that the children feel as if they were suffocating. Is a balance possible?

[3] Yes, it is. Being extreme is ineffective and can invite disaster. (Ecclesiastes 7:16, 17) But how do Christian parents find the right balance in protecting their family? Consider three areas: education, association, and recreation.

WHO WILL TEACH YOUR CHILDREN?

[4] Christian parents place a high value on educa-

1-3. (a) From what sources do destructive influences that threaten the family come? (b) What balance do parents need in protecting their family?
4. How should Christian parents view education?

tion. They know that schooling helps children to read, write, and communicate, as well as to solve problems. It should also teach them how to learn. The skills children acquire in school can help them to succeed despite the challenges of today's world. Additionally, a good education may help them to perform superior work. —Proverbs 22:29.

⁵ However, school also brings children together with other children —many of whom have distorted views. For example, consider their views on sex and morals. In a secondary school in Nigeria, a sexually promiscuous girl used to advise her fellow students about sex. They listened to her eagerly, even though her ideas were full of nonsense that she had gleaned from pornographic literature. Some of the girls experimented with her advice. As a result, one girl got pregnant out of wedlock and died of a self-induced abortion.

5, 6. How may children at school be exposed to distorted information on sexual matters?

[6] Sad to say, some of the sexual misinformation at school comes, not from children, but from teachers. Many parents are dismayed when schools teach children about sex without presenting information on moral standards and responsibility. Said the mother of a 12-year-old girl: "We live in a very religious, conservative area, and yet right in the local high school, they're handing out condoms to the kids!" She and her husband became concerned when they learned that their daughter was getting sexual propositions from boys her own age. How can parents protect their family from such wrong influences?

[7] Is it best to shield children from any mention of sexual matters? No. It is better to teach your children about sex yourself. (Proverbs 5:1) True, in parts of Europe and North America, many parents shy away from this subject. Similarly, in some African lands, parents rarely discuss sex with their children. "It's not part of African culture to do so," says a father in Sierra Leone. Some parents feel that to teach children about sex is to give them ideas that will lead them to commit immorality! But what is God's view?

GOD'S VIEW OF SEX

[8] The Bible makes it clear that there is nothing shameful about discussing sex in a proper context. In Israel, God's people were told to gather together, including their "little ones," to listen to the reading aloud of the Mosaic Law. (Deuteronomy 31: 10-12; Joshua 8:35) The Law frankly mentioned a

---

7. How may sexual misinformation be best countered?
8, 9. What fine information on sexual matters is found in the Bible?

number of sexual matters, including menstruation, seminal emissions, fornication, adultery, homosexuality, incest, and bestiality. (Leviticus 15:16, 19; 18:6, 22, 23; Deuteronomy 22:22) After such readings parents no doubt had much to explain to their inquisitive youngsters.

[9] There are passages in the fifth, sixth, and seventh chapters of Proverbs that convey loving parental counsel on the dangers of sexual immorality. These verses show that immorality may be tempting at times. (Proverbs 5:3; 6:24, 25; 7:14-21) But they teach that it is wrong and has disastrous consequences, and they offer guidance to help young people avoid immoral ways. (Proverbs 5:1-14, 21-23; 6:27-35; 7:22-27) Furthermore, immorality is contrasted with the satisfaction of sexual pleasure in its proper setting, within marriage. (Proverbs 5:15-20) What a fine model of teaching for parents to follow!

[10] Does such teaching lead children to commit immorality? On the contrary, the Bible teaches: "By knowledge are the righteous rescued." (Proverbs 11:9) Do you not want to rescue your children from this world's influences? One father said: "Ever since the children were very young, we've tried to be totally frank with them when it comes to sex. That way, when they hear other children talking about sex, they're not curious. There's no big mystery."

[11] As noted in earlier chapters, sex education should start early. When teaching little children to name body parts, do not skip over their private parts

10. Why should giving children godly knowledge about sex not lead them to commit immorality?
11. How can children be taught progressively about the intimate matters of life?

as if these were somehow shameful. Teach them the proper names for these. As time passes, lessons about privacy and boundaries are essential. Preferably both parents should teach the children that these parts of the body are special, generally not to be touched by or exposed to others, and are never to be discussed in a bad way. As children grow older, they should be informed as to how a man and a woman come together to conceive a child. By the time that their own bodies begin to enter puberty, they should already be well aware of the changes to be expected. As was discussed in Chapter 5, such education can also help to protect children from sexual abuse.—Proverbs 2:10-14.

HOMEWORK THAT PARENTS HAVE

[12] Parents need to be ready to counteract other false ideas that may be taught at school—worldly philosophies such as evolution, nationalism, or the idea that no truths are absolute. (1 Corinthians 3:19; compare Genesis 1:27; Leviticus 26:1; John 4:24; 17:17.) Many sincere school officials attach undue importance to further education. While the matter of supplementary education is a personal choice, some teachers hold that it is the only route to any personal success.*—Psalm 146:3-6.

[13] If parents are to counteract wrong or distorted teachings, they have to know just what instruction

---

* For a discussion of supplementary education, see the brochure *Jehovah's Witnesses and Education,* published by the Watchtower Bible and Tract Society of New York, Inc., pages 4-7.

12. What distorted views are often taught in schools?
13. How can children attending school be protected from wrong ideas?

their children are receiving. So parents, remember that you have homework too! Show a genuine interest in your children's schooling. Talk with them after school. Ask what they are learning, what they like most, what they find most challenging. Look over homework assignments, notes, and test results. Try to get to know their teachers. Let teachers know that you appreciate their work and that you want to be of help in any way you can.

YOUR CHILDREN'S FRIENDS

[14] "Where on earth did you learn that?" How many parents have asked that question, horrified at something that their child has said or done and that seems completely out of character? And how often does the answer involve some new friend at school or in the neighborhood? Yes, companions affect us profoundly, whether we are young or old. The apostle Paul warned: "Do not be misled. Bad associations spoil useful habits." (1 Corinthians 15:33; Proverbs 13:20) Youths in particular are susceptible to peer pressure. They tend to be uncertain about themselves and may at times feel overwhelmed by a desire to please and impress their associates. How vital it is, then, that they choose good friends!

[15] As every parent knows, children will not always choose well; they need some guidance. It is not a matter of choosing their friends for them. Rather, as they grow, teach them discernment and help them to see what qualities they should value in friends. The main quality is a love of Jehovah and of doing

---

14. Why is it vital that godly children choose good friends?
15. How can parents guide their children in choosing friends?

what is right in his eyes. (Mark 12:28-30) Teach them to love and respect those who possess honesty, kindness, generosity, diligence. During the family study, help children to recognize such qualities in Bible characters and then to find the same traits in others in the congregation. Set the example by using the same criteria in choosing your own friends.

¹⁶ Do you know who your children's friends are? Why not have your children bring them home so that you can meet them? You might also ask your children what other children think about these friends. Are they known for demonstrating personal integrity or for living a double life? If the latter is true, help your children to reason on why such association could hurt them. (Psalm 26:4, 5, 9-12) If you notice undesirable changes in your child's behavior, dress, attitude, or speech, you may need to have a talk about his or her friends. Your child may be spending time with a friend who is exerting a negative influence.—Compare Genesis 34:1, 2.

¹⁷ Yet it is not enough simply to teach your children to avoid bad associates. Help them to find good ones. One father says: "We would always try to substitute. So when the school wanted our son on the football team, my wife and I sat down with him and discussed why that wouldn't be a good idea—because of the new companions that would be involved. But then we suggested getting some of the other children in the congregation and taking all of them to the park to play ball. And that worked out fine."

16. How may parents watch their children's choice of friends?
17, 18. Besides warning against bad associates, what practical help can parents give?

HE DID NOT FEEL DEPRIVED

Christian parents Paul and his wife, Lu-Ann, organize gatherings at their home from time to time. They make sure that the gatherings are well supervised and of a manageable size. They have good reason to believe that their children benefit.

Lu-Ann relates: "The mother of a classmate of my six-year-old son, Eric, approached me to say that she felt sorry for Eric because he sat apart and didn't join in class birthday parties. I said to her: 'I really appreciate that you care about my son that way. It says a lot about the kind of person you are. And probably there is nothing I could say that would convince you that Eric doesn't feel that he's missing out.' She agreed. So I said: 'Then please, for your own sake, set your mind at ease and ask Eric yourself how he feels.' When I was not around, she asked Eric, 'Don't you mind missing out on these nice birthday parties?' He looked up at her, surprised, and said: 'Do you think that ten minutes, a few cupcakes, and a song make a party? You should come to my house and see what a real party is like!'" The boy's innocent enthusiasm made it clear—he did not feel that he was deprived or missing out!

[18] Wise parents help their children to find good friends and then to enjoy wholesome recreation with them. For many parents, though, this matter of recreation presents challenges of its own.

WHAT KIND OF RECREATION?

[19] Does the Bible condemn having fun? Far from

---

19. What Bible examples show that it is not sinful for families to have fun?

it! The Bible says that there is "a time to laugh . . . and a time to skip about."* (Ecclesiastes 3:4) God's people in ancient Israel enjoyed music and dancing, games, and riddles. Jesus Christ attended a large wedding feast and "a big reception feast" that Matthew Levi put on for him. (Luke 5:29; John 2:1, 2) Clearly, Jesus was no killjoy. May laughter and fun never be viewed as sins in your household!

[20] Jehovah is "the happy God." (1 Timothy 1:11) So worship of Jehovah should be a source of delight, not something that casts a shadow of joylessness over life. (Compare Deuteronomy 16:15.) Children are naturally exuberant and full of energy that can be released in play and recreation. Well-chosen recreation is more than fun. It is a way for a child to learn and mature. A family head is responsible to provide for his household's needs in everything, including recreation. However, balance is required.

[21] In these troubled "last days," human society is filled with people who are "lovers of pleasures rather than lovers of God," just as was prophesied in the Bible. (2 Timothy 3:1-5) For many, recreation is the main thing in life. There is so much entertainment available that it can easily crowd out more important things. Further, much modern entertainment features sexual immorality, violence, drug abuse, and other grossly harmful practices. (Proverbs 3:31)

---

* The Hebrew word here rendered "to laugh" can, in other forms, be rendered "to play," "to offer some amusement," "to celebrate," or even "to have fun."

---

20. What should parents bear in mind in providing recreation for the family?
21. What pitfalls exist in recreation today?

Well-chosen recreation, such as this family camping trip, can help children to learn and to grow spiritually

What can be done to safeguard youngsters from harmful entertainment?

[22] Parents need to set boundaries and restrictions. But more than that, they need to teach their children how to judge what recreation is harmful and to know how much is too much. Such training takes time and effort. Consider an example. A father of two boys noticed that his older son was listening to a new radio station quite frequently. So while driving his truck to work one day, the father tuned in to the same station. Occasionally he stopped and jotted down the lyrics of certain songs. Later he sat down with his

---

22. How can parents train their children to make wise decisions as to recreation?

sons and discussed what he had heard. He asked viewpoint questions, beginning with "What do you think?" and listened patiently to their answers. After reasoning on the matter using the Bible, the boys agreed not to listen to that station.

²³ Wise Christian parents check the music, TV programs, videotapes, comic books, video games, and movies that interest their children. They look at the art on the cover, the lyrics, and the packaging, and they read newspaper reviews and watch excerpts. Many are shocked at some of the "entertainment" directed at children today. Those who wish to protect their children from unclean influences sit down with the family and discuss the dangers, using the Bible and Bible-based publications, such as the book *Questions Young People Ask—Answers That Work* and articles in the *Watchtower* and *Awake!* magazines.* When parents set firm limits, being consistent and reasonable, they usually see good results.—Matthew 5:37; Philippians 4:5.

²⁴ Of course, restricting harmful forms of recreation is only part of the battle. The bad must be countered by the good, otherwise children may drift into a wrong course. Many Christian families have countless warm and happy memories of enjoying recreation together—picnicking, hiking, camping, playing games and sports, traveling to visit relatives or friends. Some have found that simply reading

_____

* Published by the Watchtower Bible and Tract Society of New York, Inc.

23. How may parents protect their children from unwholesome entertainment?
24, 25. What are some wholesome forms of recreation that families can enjoy together?

aloud together for relaxation is a great source of pleasure and comfort. Others enjoy telling humorous or interesting stories. Still others have developed hobbies together, for example, woodworking and other crafts, as well as playing musical instruments, painting, or studying God's creations. Children who learn to enjoy such diversions are protected from much unclean entertainment, and they learn that there is more to recreation than simply sitting passively and being entertained. Participating is often more fun than observing.

[25] Social gatherings can also be a rewarding form of recreation. When they are well supervised and not outlandishly large or time-consuming, they can give your children more than just fun. They can help to deepen the bonds of love in the congregation.—Compare Luke 14:13, 14; Jude 12.

YOUR FAMILY CAN CONQUER THE WORLD

[26] Without question, protecting your family from the world's destructive influences requires much hard work. But there is one thing that, more than any other, will make success possible. It is love! Close, loving family bonds will make your home a safe haven and will promote communication, which is a great protection from bad influences. Further, cultivating another kind of love is even more important—love of Jehovah. When such love permeates the family, the children are more likely to grow up hating the very idea of displeasing God by succumbing to worldly influences. And parents who love Jehovah from the heart will seek to imitate his loving,

---

26. When it comes to protecting the family from unwholesome influences, what is the most important quality?

reasonable, balanced personality. (Ephesians 5:1; James 3:17) If parents do that, their children will have no reason to view worship of Jehovah as just a list of things they are not allowed to do or as a way of life devoid of fun or laughter, from which they want to run away as soon as possible. Rather, they will see that worshiping God is the happiest, fullest way of life possible.

27 Families that stay united in happy, balanced service to God, endeavoring wholeheartedly to remain "spotless and unblemished" from the corrupting influences of this world, are a source of joy to Jehovah. (2 Peter 3:14; Proverbs 27:11) Such families follow in the footsteps of Jesus Christ, who resisted every effort of Satan's world to defile him. Near the end of his human life, Jesus was able to say: "I have conquered the world." (John 16:33) May your family also conquer the world and enjoy life forever!

27. How can a family conquer the world?

HOW CAN THESE BIBLE PRINCIPLES HELP... TO PROTECT YOUR FAMILY?

Knowledge leads to wisdom, which can preserve a person alive.—Ecclesiastes 7:12.

"The wisdom of this world is foolishness with God."—1 Corinthians 3:19.

Bad associations must be avoided. —1 Corinthians 15:33.

While recreation has its place, it should be controlled.—Ecclesiastes 3:4.

CHAPTER NINE

Single-Parent Families Can Succeed!

ONE-PARENT families have been called "the fastest growing family style" in the United States. The situation is similar in many other lands. A record number of divorces, desertions, separations, and illegitimate births have had far-reaching consequences for millions of parents and children.

[2] "I am a 28-year-old widow with two children," wrote one single mother. "I am very depressed for I don't want to raise my children without a father. It seems like no one even cares about me. My children see me cry often and it affects them." Besides wrestling with such feelings as anger, guilt, and loneliness, most single parents face the challenge of both holding a job outside the home and performing domestic duties. One said: "Being a single parent is like being a juggler. After six months of practice, you have finally been able to juggle four balls at once. But just as soon as you are able to do that, somebody throws a new ball to you!"

[3] Youngsters in single-parent families often have their own struggles. They may have to contend with intense emotions in the wake of a parent's abrupt departure or death. For many youths the absence of a parent seems to have a profoundly negative effect.

1-3. What has led to the growth in the number of single-parent families, and how are those involved affected?

⁴ One-parent families existed in Bible times. The Scriptures repeatedly mention the "fatherless boy" and the "widow." (Exodus 22:22; Deuteronomy 24: 19-21; Job 31:16-22) Jehovah God was not indifferent to their plight. The psalmist called God "a father of fatherless boys and a judge of widows." (Psalm 68:5) Surely, Jehovah has the same concern for one-parent families today! Indeed, his Word offers principles that can help them to succeed.

MASTERING THE HOUSEHOLD ROUTINE

⁵ Consider the task of managing a home. "There are many occasions when you wish you had a man around," admits one divorcée, "like when your car starts making noises and you don't know where they are coming from." Men who are recently divorced or widowed may likewise be bewildered by the multitude of household tasks they must now perform. For children, domestic disarray adds to feelings of instability and insecurity.

⁶ What can help? Note the example set by the "capable wife" described at Proverbs 31:10-31. The breadth of her accomplishments is remarkable —buying, selling, sewing, cooking, investing in real estate, farming, and managing a business. Her secret? She was diligent, working late and getting up early to start her activities. And she was well organized, delegating some tasks and using her own hands to care for others. No wonder she won praise!

4. How do we know that Jehovah is concerned about single-parent families?
5. What problem do single parents have to face initially?
6, 7. (a) What fine example was set by the "capable wife" of Proverbs? (b) How does being diligent about domestic responsibilities help in single-parent homes?

⁷ If you are a single parent, be conscientious about your domestic responsibilities. Find satisfaction in such work, for this does much to add to the happiness of your children. However, proper planning and organization are essential. The Bible says: "The plans of the diligent one surely make for advantage." (Proverbs 21:5) One single father admitted: "I tend not to think about meals until I'm hungry." But planned meals tend to be more nutritious and appealing than those hastily improvised. You may also have to learn to use your hands in new ways. By consulting knowledgeable friends, how-to books, and helpful professionals, some single mothers have been able to tackle painting, plumbing, and simple auto repairs.

⁸ Is it fair to ask children to help out? One single mother reasoned: "You want to make up for the absence of the other parent by making it easy for the children." That may be understandable but perhaps not always in the best interests of the child. God-fearing youths of Bible times were assigned appropriate chores. (Genesis 37:2; Song of Solomon 1:6) So, although being careful not to overload your children, you will be wise to assign them tasks such as taking care of the dishes and keeping their room clean. Why not perform some chores together? This can be very enjoyable.

THE CHALLENGE OF MAKING A LIVING

⁹ Most single parents find it difficult to meet their financial needs, and young unwed mothers usually

---

8. How can children of single parents help out in the home?
9. Why do single mothers often face financial hardships?

have a particularly hard time.* In lands where public assistance is available, they may be wise to make use of it, at least until they can find employment. The Bible permits Christians to utilize such provisions when necessary. (Romans 13:1, 6) Widows and divorcées face similar challenges. Many, forced to reenter the job market after years of homemaking, can often find only low-paying work. Some manage to improve their lot by enrolling in job-training programs or short-term school courses.

¹⁰ Do not be surprised if your children are unhappy when you seek employment, and do not feel guilty. Rather, explain to them why you must work, and help them to understand that Jehovah requires you to provide for them. (1 Timothy 5:8) In time, most children adjust. However, try to spend as much time with them as your busy schedule allows. Such loving attention can also help to minimize the impact of any financial limitations the family may experience.—Proverbs 15:16, 17.

WHO IS TAKING CARE OF WHOM?

¹¹ It is natural for single parents to be especially close to their children, yet care must be taken that the God-assigned boundaries between parents and children do not break down. For example, serious difficulties can arise if a single mother expects her

---

* If a young Christian becomes pregnant because of immoral conduct, the Christian congregation in no way condones what she has done. But if she is repentant, congregation elders and others in the congregation may wish to offer her help.

---

10. How can a single mother explain to her children why she must find secular employment?
11, 12. What boundaries must single parents preserve, and how can they do so?

Spend as much time as possible with your children

son to take on the responsibilities of the man of the house or treats her daughter as a confidant, burdening the girl with intimate problems. Doing so is inappropriate, stressful, and perhaps confusing to a child.

¹² Assure your children that you, as the parent, will care for them—not vice versa. (Compare 2 Corinthians 12:14.) At times, you may need some advice or support. Seek it from Christian elders or perhaps from mature Christian women, not from your minor children.—Titus 2:3.

MAINTAINING DISCIPLINE

¹³ A man may have little trouble being taken

13. What problem regarding discipline may a single mother face?

seriously as a disciplinarian, but a woman may have problems in this regard. Says one single mother: "My sons have men's bodies and men's voices. Sometimes it is hard not to sound indecisive or weak in comparison." Furthermore, you may still be grieving over the death of a beloved mate, or perhaps you may be feeling guilt or anger over a marital breakup. If there is shared custody, you may fear that your child prefers being with your former mate. Such situations can make it difficult to administer balanced discipline.

[14] The Bible says that "a boy let on the loose will be causing his mother shame." (Proverbs 29:15) You have the backing of Jehovah God in making and enforcing family rules, so do not give in to guilt, remorse, or fear. (Proverbs 1:8) Never compromise Bible principles. (Proverbs 13:24) Try to be reasonable, consistent, and firm. In time, most children will respond. Still, you will want to take the feelings of your children into consideration. Says one single father: "My discipline had to be tempered with understanding because of the shock of losing their mother. I talk to them at every opportunity. We have 'cozy moments' when we prepare dinner. It is then that they really confide in me."

[15] If you are divorced, nothing good is accomplished by undermining respect for your former mate. Parental bickering is painful for children and will ultimately weaken their respect for both of you. Hence, avoid making hurtful remarks like: "You're

---

14. How can single parents maintain a balanced view of discipline?
15. What should a divorced parent avoid when speaking of the ex-mate?

FAMILY HAPPINESS

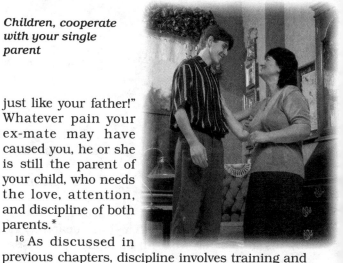

Children, cooperate with your single parent

just like your father!" Whatever pain your ex-mate may have caused you, he or she is still the parent of your child, who needs the love, attention, and discipline of both parents.*

¹⁶ As discussed in previous chapters, discipline involves training and instruction, not just punishment. Many problems can be averted by a good program of spiritual training. (Philippians 3:16) Regular attendance at Christian meetings is essential. (Hebrews 10:24, 25) So is having a weekly family Bible study. True, it is not easy to keep such a study going. "After a day's work, you really want to relax," says one conscientious mother. "But I prepare myself mentally to study with my daughter, knowing it is something that needs to be done. She really enjoys our family study!"

---

* We are not referring to situations in which a child may need to be protected from an abusive parent. Also, if the other parent tries to weaken *your* authority, perhaps with a view to persuading the children to leave you, it may be well to speak to experienced friends, such as the elders in the Christian congregation, for advice concerning how to handle the situation.

16. What spiritual arrangements should be a regular part of discipline in a single-parent home?

The congregation does not ignore "widows" and "fatherless boys"

¹⁷ The apostle Paul's companion Timothy was evidently given his training in Bible principles by his mother and his grandmother—but apparently not by his father. Yet, what an outstanding Christian Timothy became! (Acts 16:1, 2; 2 Timothy 1:5; 3: 14, 15) You can likewise hope for favorable results as you strive to raise your children "in the discipline and mental-regulating of Jehovah."—Ephesians 6:4.

WINNING THE BATTLE AGAINST LONELINESS

¹⁸ One single parent sighed: "When I come home and see those four walls, and especially after the children are in bed, loneliness really comes over me." Yes, loneliness is often the biggest problem a single parent faces. It is natural to long for the warm companionship and intimacies of marriage. But should a person try to solve this problem at any cost? In the apostle Paul's day, some younger widows allowed "their sexual impulses [to] come be-

17. What can we learn from the fine upbringing of Paul's companion Timothy?
18, 19. (a) How can loneliness manifest itself for a single parent? (b) What counsel is given to help control fleshly desires?

tween them and the Christ." (1 Timothy 5:11, 12) Permitting fleshly desires to overshadow spiritual interests would be damaging.—1 Timothy 5:6.

[19] A Christian man said: "Sexual urges are very strong, but you can control them. When a thought comes into your mind, you must not dwell on it. You have to get rid of it. It also helps to think of your child." God's Word counsels: 'Deaden your body members as respects sexual appetite.' (Colossians 3:5) If you were trying to deaden your appetite for food, would you read magazines featuring pictures of delicious foods, or would you associate with people who constantly talked about food? Hardly! The same is true concerning fleshly desires.

[20] Some Christians have entered into courtships with unbelievers. (1 Corinthians 7:39) Did that solve their problem? No. A divorced Christian woman warned: "There is one thing much worse than being single. It is being married to the wrong person!" First-century Christian widows no doubt had bouts of loneliness, but the wise ones kept busy 'entertaining strangers, washing the feet of the holy ones, and relieving those in tribulation.' (1 Timothy 5:10) Faithful Christians today who have waited many years to find a God-fearing mate have similarly kept busy. A 68-year-old Christian widow started visiting other widows whenever she got lonely. She said: "I find that by making these visits, keeping up my housework and taking care of my spirituality I don't have time to be lonely." Teaching

---

20. (a) What danger lurks for those who court unbelievers? (b) How have single people both in the first century and today battled loneliness?

WHAT YOUNG ONES CAN DO

Is your mother or father a single parent? If so, what can you do to help? For one thing, be obedient. Neither size nor gender gives a child the license to 'forsake the law of his mother.' (Proverbs 1:8) Jehovah commands you to be obedient, and in the long run, doing so will work for your happiness.—Proverbs 23:22; Ephesians 6:1-3.

Take the initiative, and be appreciative. "My mother works in a hospital, and her uniform has to be pressed. So I iron it for her," says Tony. "It helps my mom, so I do it." One single mother says: "I often find that when I am really low or irritable from a particularly trying day at work and I come home—that is the day my daughter has chosen to set the table and get the supper going."

Keep in mind that your cooperation is important. After a hard day's work, it may be difficult for your parent to conduct a family Bible study. If you are uncooperative, you make matters worse. Try to be ready when the scheduled time arrives. Prepare your lessons beforehand. By being obedient, appreciative, and cooperative, you will please your parent, and even more important, you will please God.

others about God's Kingdom is an especially beneficial good work.—Matthew 28:19, 20.

[21] Admittedly, there is no miracle cure for loneliness. But it can be endured with strength from Jehovah. Such strength comes when a Christian "persists in supplications and prayers night and day." (1 Timothy 5:5) Supplications are earnest pleas, yes,

---

21. In what way can prayer and good association help overcome loneliness?

a begging for help, perhaps with strong outcries and tears. (Compare Hebrews 5:7.) Pouring out your heart to Jehovah "night and day" can really help. Further, wholesome association can do much to fill the void of loneliness. Through good association, one can get "the good word" of encouragement described at Proverbs 12:25.

²² If feelings of loneliness surface from time to time—as they likely will—remember that no one has a perfect lot in life. Indeed, "the entire association of your brothers" is suffering in one way or another. (1 Peter 5:9) Avoid dwelling on the past. (Ecclesiastes 7:10) Take stock of the advantages that you enjoy. Above all, be determined to keep your integrity and to make Jehovah's heart glad.—Proverbs 27:11.

HOW OTHERS CAN HELP

²³ The support and help of fellow Christians is invaluable. James 1:27 says: "The form of worship that is clean and undefiled from the standpoint of our God and Father is this: to look after orphans and widows in their tribulation." Yes, Christians are obliged to assist single-parent families. What are some practical ways in which this might be done?

²⁴ Material help can be given. The Bible says: "Whoever has this world's means for supporting life and beholds his brother having need and yet shuts the door of his tender compassions upon

---

22. What considerations will help when feelings of loneliness surface from time to time?
23. What responsibility do fellow Christians have toward single parents in the congregation?
24. In what ways may needy single-parent families be helped?

him, in what way does the love of God remain in him?" (1 John 3:17) The original Greek word for "beholds" means, not just a casual glance, but a deliberate gaze. This indicates that a kindly Christian might first become familiar with a family's circumstances and needs. Perhaps they are in need of money. Some may need help with household repairs. Or they might simply appreciate being invited over for a meal or a social gathering.

25 In addition, 1 Peter 3:8 says: "All of you be likeminded, showing fellow feeling, having brotherly affection, tenderly compassionate." Said one single parent with six children: "It's been hard and sometimes I get weighed down. However, once in a while one of the brothers or sisters will say to me: 'Joan, you're doing a good job. It's going to be worth it.' Just to know that others are thinking of you and that they care is so helpful." Older Christian women may be particularly effective in helping young women who are single parents, offering them a listening ear when they have problems that might be awkward for them to discuss with a man.

26 Christian men can help out in other ways. The righteous man Job said: "I would rescue . . . the fatherless boy and anyone that had no helper." (Job 29:12) Some Christian men today likewise take a wholesome interest in fatherless children and show genuine "love out of a clean heart," having no ulterior motives. (1 Timothy 1:5) Without neglecting their own families, they might occasionally ar-

25. How may fellow Christians show compassion toward single parents?
26. How can mature Christian men help fatherless children?

range to work with such young ones in the Christian ministry and might also invite them to share in family study or in recreation. Such kindness could very well rescue a fatherless child from a wayward course.

²⁷ Ultimately, of course, single parents have to 'carry their own load' of responsibility. (Galatians 6:5) Nevertheless, they can have the love of Christian brothers and sisters and of Jehovah God himself. The Bible says of him: "The fatherless boy and the widow he relieves." (Psalm 146:9) With His loving support, single-parent families can succeed!

---

27. Of what support can single parents be assured?

HOW CAN THESE BIBLE PRINCIPLES HELP...
PARENTS AND CHILDREN TO HANDLE THE
PROBLEMS OF SINGLE-PARENT FAMILIES?

Jehovah God is "a father of
fatherless boys and a judge of widows."
—Psalm 68:5.

Proper planning is essential for success.
—Proverbs 21:5.

Jehovah supports the parent's right to give
proper discipline.—Proverbs 1:8.

Wise Christian widows keep busy
in good works and persist in prayer.
—1 Timothy 5:5, 10.

Showing a proper interest in "orphans and
widows" is a part of true worship.—James 1:27.

CHAPTER TEN

When a Family Member Is Sick

THE man Job must surely be counted among those who enjoyed a happy family life. The Bible calls him "the greatest of all the Orientals." He had seven sons and three daughters, ten children in all. He also had the means to provide well for his family. Most important, he took the lead in spiritual activities and was concerned about his children's standing before Jehovah. All of this resulted in close and happy family ties.—Job 1:1-5.

² Job's situation did not escape the attention of Satan, Jehovah God's archenemy. Satan, who is constantly looking for ways to break the integrity of God's servants, attacked Job by destroying his happy family. Then, he "struck Job with a malignant boil from the sole of his foot to the crown of his head." Thus Satan hoped to use tragedy and sickness to break Job's integrity.—Job 2:6, 7.

³ The Bible does not give the medical designation of Job's affliction. It does, though, tell us the symptoms. His flesh was covered with maggots, and his skin formed crusts and rotted away. Job's breath was loathsome, and his body was foul smelling. He was racked with pain. (Job 7:5; 19:17; 30:17, 30) In agony Job sat among the ashes and scraped him-

---

1, 2. How did Satan use tragedy and sickness to try to break Job's integrity?

3. What were the symptoms of Job's illness?

self with a piece of broken earthenware. (Job 2:8) Truly a pitiable sight!

⁴ How would you react if you were afflicted with such a serious disease? Today, Satan does not strike God's servants with sickness as he did Job. Still, in view of human imperfection, the stresses of daily life, and the deteriorating environment we live in, it is only to be expected that from time to time, family members will get sick. Despite the preventive measures that we might take, all of us are susceptible to illness, although few will suffer to the extent that Job did. When sickness invades our household, it can truly be a challenge. Let us therefore see how the Bible helps us to cope with this ever-present enemy of mankind.—Ecclesiastes 9:11; 2 Timothy 3:16.

HOW DO YOU FEEL ABOUT IT?

⁵ Disruption of the normal routine of life, no matter what the cause, is always difficult, and this is especially true if the disruption is caused by prolonged sickness. Even a short-term illness calls for adjustments, concessions, and sacrifices. Healthy family members may have to keep quiet to allow the sick one to get rest. They may have to forgo certain activities. Still, in most families even young children feel compassion for a sick sibling or parent, although they may occasionally have to be reminded to be thoughtful. (Colossians 3:12) In the case of temporary sickness, the family is usually ready to do what is needed. Besides, each family member would hope for similar consideration if he or she

---

4. What experience does every family have from time to time?
5. How do family members usually react in cases of temporary sickness?

Christians show the depth of their love when their partners fall sick

were to get sick.—Matthew 7:12.

⁶ What, though, if the illness is very serious and the disruptions are drastic and prolonged? For example, what if someone in the family is paralyzed by a stroke, disabled by Alzheimer's disease, or debilitated by some other illness? Or what if a member of the family is afflicted with a mental illness, such as schizophrenia? A common initial reaction is pity—sadness that a loved one is suffering so much. However, pity may be followed by other reactions. As family members find themselves very much affected and their freedoms limited by the sickness of one person, they may come to feel resentment. They may wonder: "Why does this have to happen to me?"

⁷ Something similar seems to have gone through the mind of Job's wife. Remember, she had already experienced the loss of her children. As those tragic events unfolded, she no doubt felt progressively more distraught. Finally, as she saw her once active and vigorous husband afflicted with a painful,

6. What reactions are sometimes seen if a family member is struck with a serious, lasting sickness?
7. How did Job's wife react to his sickness, and what did she evidently forget?

FAMILY HAPPINESS

loathsome disease, she appears to have lost sight of the vital factor that overshadowed all the tragedies —the relationship that she and her husband had with God. The Bible says: "Finally [Job's] wife said to him: 'Are you yet holding fast your integrity? Curse God and die!' "—Job 2:9.

⁸ Many feel frustrated, even angry, when their life is radically changed by someone else's sickness. Still, a Christian who reasons on the situation should realize eventually that this affords him an opportunity to demonstrate the genuineness of his love. True love "is long-suffering and kind . . . [and] does not look for its own interests . . . It bears all things, believes all things, hopes all things, endures all things." (1 Corinthians 13:4-7) Rather than allow negative feelings to dominate, therefore, it is essential that we do our best to get them under control. —Proverbs 3:21.

⁹ What can be done to safeguard the spiritual and emotional welfare of a family when one of its members is seriously ill? Of course, each illness calls for its own particular care and treatment, and it would not be proper in this publication to recommend any medical or home-care procedures. Nonetheless, in a spiritual sense, Jehovah "is raising up all who are bowed down." (Psalm 145:14) King David wrote: "Happy is anyone acting with consideration toward the lowly one; in the day of calamity Jehovah will provide escape for him. Jehovah himself will guard him and preserve him alive. . . . Jehovah himself

---

8. When a family member is very sick, what scripture will help other family members to keep a proper viewpoint?
9. What assurances can help a family spiritually and emotionally when a member is seriously ill?

will sustain him upon a divan of illness." (Psalm 41: 1-3) Jehovah preserves his servants alive spiritually, even when they are tried emotionally beyond their own limits. (2 Corinthians 4:7) Many family members facing serious sickness in their household have echoed the words of the psalmist: "I have been afflicted to a great extent. O Jehovah, preserve me alive according to your word."—Psalm 119:107.

A HEALING SPIRIT

[10] "The spirit of a man can put up with his malady," says a Bible proverb, "but as for a stricken spirit, who can bear it?" (Proverbs 18:14) Trauma can afflict the spirit of a family as well as "the spirit of a man." Yet, "a calm heart is the life of the fleshly organism." (Proverbs 14:30) Whether a family successfully copes with serious illness or not depends to a large extent on the attitude, or spirit, of its members.—Compare Proverbs 17:22.

[11] One Christian woman had to endure seeing her husband impaired by a stroke only six years after they were married. "My husband's speech was badly affected, and it became almost impossible to converse with him," she recalled. "The mental strain of trying to understand what he was struggling to say was very great." Imagine, too, the agony and frustration that the husband must have experienced. What did the couple do? Even though they lived a long way from the Christian congregation, the sister did her best to stay spiritually strong by keeping up-to-date with all the latest organizational infor-

10, 11. (a) What is vital if a family is to cope successfully with sickness? (b) How did one woman cope with the sickness of her husband?

mation as well as with the continual supply of spiritual food in the *Watchtower* and *Awake!* magazines. This gave her the spiritual strength to care for her dear husband until his death four years later.

¹² In Job's case it was he, the one afflicted, who remained strong. "Shall we accept merely what is good from the true God and not accept also what is bad?" he asked his wife. (Job 2:10) No wonder the disciple James later cited Job as an outstanding example of patience and forbearance! At James 5:11 we read: "You have heard of the endurance of Job and have seen the outcome Jehovah gave, that Jehovah is very tender in affection and merciful." Similarly today, in many cases the courageous attitude of the sick family member has helped others in the household to maintain a positive outlook.

¹³ Most who have had to deal with sickness in the family agree that initially it is not unusual for family members to have a difficult time facing the facts. They also point out that the way in which one comes to view the situation is extremely important. Changes and adjustments in the household routine may be difficult at the outset. But if a person really makes the effort, he can adapt to a new situation. In doing so, it is important that we not compare our circumstances with those of others who do not have sickness in the family, thinking that their life is easier and that 'it is just not fair!' Actually, no one really knows what burdens others have to bear. All Christians find comfort in Jesus' words: "Come to me,

---

12. As seen in the case of Job, what contribution does the sick one sometimes make?
13. What comparison should not be made by a family experiencing serious sickness?

all you who are toiling and loaded down, and I will refresh you."—Matthew 11:28.

SETTING PRIORITIES

¹⁴ In the face of serious sickness, a family would do well to remember the inspired words: "In the multitude of counselors there is accomplishment." (Proverbs 15:22) Could family members come together and discuss the situation caused by the sickness? It would certainly be appropriate to do so prayerfully and to turn to God's Word for guidance. (Psalm 25:4) What should be considered in such a discussion? Well, there are medical, financial, and family decisions to be made. Who will provide the primary care? How can the family cooperate to support that care? How will the arrangements made affect each member of the family? How will the spiritual and other needs of the primary caregiver be looked after?

¹⁵ Praying earnestly for Jehovah's direction, meditating on his Word, and courageously following the way indicated by the Bible often result in blessings beyond our expectations. The disease of an ailing family member may not always go into remission. But leaning on Jehovah always leads to the best outcome in any situation. (Psalm 55:22) The psalmist wrote: "Your own loving-kindness, O Jehovah, kept sustaining me. When my disquieting thoughts became many inside of me, your own consolations began to fondle my soul."—Psalm 94:18, 19; see also Psalm 63:6-8.

14. How can proper priorities be set?
15. What support does Jehovah provide for families experiencing serious sickness?

FAMILY HAPPINESS

HELPING THE CHILDREN

¹⁶ Serious sickness can cause problems for children in the family. It is important that parents help the children to understand the needs that have arisen and what they may do to help. If the one who has become ill is a child, the siblings must be helped to understand that the extra attention and care the sick one is receiving does not mean that the other children are loved any less. Rather than allow resentment or rivalry to develop, parents can help the other children to form a closer bond with one another and have genuine affection as they cooperate in handling the situation caused by the sickness.

¹⁷ Young children will usually respond more readily if parents appeal to their feelings rather than to lengthy or complicated explanations about medical conditions. So they could be given some idea of what the sick family member is going through. If the healthy children see how the illness prevents the sick one from doing many of the things that they themselves take for granted, they are likely to have more "brotherly affection" and to be "tenderly compassionate."—1 Peter 3:8.

¹⁸ Older children should be helped to realize that a difficult situation exists and it requires sacrifices on the part of everyone in the family. With doctors' fees and medical bills to pay, it may not be possible for parents to provide for the other children

---

16, 17. What points can be made when discussing with young children the sickness of a sibling?
18. How can older children be helped to understand the problems caused by sickness, and how might this be of benefit to them?

as they would like to. Will the children resent this and feel that they are being deprived? Or will they understand the situation and be willing to make the needed sacrifices? Much depends on the way the matter is discussed and the spirit that is engendered in the family. Indeed, in many families the sickness of a family member has helped in training children to follow Paul's counsel: "[Do] nothing out of contentiousness or out of egotism, but with lowliness of mind considering that the others are superior to you, keeping an eye, not in personal interest upon just your own matters, but also in personal interest upon those of the others."—Philippians 2:3, 4.

HOW TO VIEW MEDICAL TREATMENT

[19] Balanced Christians do not object to medical treatment as long as it does not go against God's law. When a member of their family becomes ill, they are eager to seek help to relieve the suffering of the afflicted one. Still, there may be conflicting professional opinions that must be weighed. Additionally, in recent years new diseases and disorders have been cropping up, and for many of these, there is no generally accepted method of treatment. Even accurate diagnoses are sometimes difficult to obtain. What, then, should a Christian do?

[20] Although one Bible writer was a physician and the apostle Paul offered helpful medical advice to his friend Timothy, the Scriptures are a moral and spiritual guide, not a medical textbook. (Colossians

19, 20. (a) What responsibilities do family heads shoulder when a family member is sick? (b) Although not a medical textbook, in what way does the Bible provide guidance in handling sickness?

When the family works together, problems can be handled

4:14; 1 Timothy 5:23) Hence, in matters of medical treatment, Christian family heads have to make their own balanced decisions. Perhaps they may feel that they need to obtain more than one professional opinion. (Compare Proverbs 18:17.) They will certainly want the best available help for their sick family member, and most seek this among regular medical doctors. Some feel more comfortable with alternative health therapies. This too is a personal decision. Still, when handling health problems, Christians do not cease to let 'God's word be a lamp to their foot and a light to their roadway.' (Psalm 119:105) They continue to follow the guidelines set out in the Bible. (Isaiah 55:8, 9) Thus, they shun diagnostic techniques that smack of spiritism, and they avoid treatments that violate Bible principles. —Psalm 36:9; Acts 15:28, 29; Revelation 21:8.

21 Consider the case of a young Asian woman. A little while after she began to learn about the Bible as a result of studying with one of Jehovah's Witnesses, she gave birth prematurely to a baby girl who weighed only three and a quarter pounds. The woman was heartbroken when a doctor told her that the baby would be severely retarded and would never be able to walk. He advised her to surrender the baby to an institution. Her husband was uncertain about the matter. To whom could she turn?

22 She says: "I remember learning from the Bible that 'sons are an inheritance from Jehovah; the fruitage of the belly is a reward.'" (Psalm 127:3) She decided to take this "inheritance" home and to care for her. Things were difficult at first, but with the help of Christian friends in the local congregation of Jehovah's Witnesses, the woman was able to manage and to provide the child with the special support needed. Twelve years later, the child was going to the meetings at the Kingdom Hall and enjoying the company of the youngsters there. The mother comments: "I am so grateful that Bible principles moved me to do what is right. The Bible helped me to maintain a clear conscience before Jehovah God and not to have regrets that would have been with me for the rest of my life."

23 Sickness will not be with us forever. The proph-

21, 22. How did one Asian woman reason on a Bible principle, and how did the decision she made prove right in her situation?
23. What comfort does the Bible give for the sick and for those who care for them?

et Isaiah pointed forward to the time when "no resident will say: 'I am sick.'" (Isaiah 33:24) That promise will be fulfilled in the rapidly approaching new world. Until then, however, we have to live with sickness and death. Happily, God's Word gives us guidance and help. The basic rules of conduct that the Bible provides are lasting, and they transcend the ever-changing opinions of imperfect humans. Hence, a wise person agrees with the psalmist who wrote: "The law of Jehovah is perfect, bringing back the soul. The reminder of Jehovah is trustworthy, making the inexperienced one wise. . . . The judicial decisions of Jehovah are true; they have proved altogether righteous. . . . In the keeping of them there is a large reward."—Psalm 19:7, 9, 11.

HOW CAN THESE BIBLE PRINCIPLES HELP . . . A FAMILY TO HANDLE SEVERE ILLNESS AND THE DISRUPTIONS IT CAUSES?

Love is long-suffering and endures all things.
—1 Corinthians 13:4-7.

It is important to cultivate a good spirit.
—Proverbs 18:14.

It is good to seek counsel before making important decisions.—Proverbs 15:22.

Jehovah offers us support when life is difficult.
—Psalm 55:22.

Jehovah's Word is a guide in all situations.
—Psalm 119:105.

CHAPTER ELEVEN

Maintain Peace in Your Household

HAPPY are those who belong to families in which there is love, understanding, and peace. Hopefully, yours is such a family. Sad to say, countless families fail to fit that description and are divided for one reason or another. What divides households? In this chapter we will discuss three things. In some families, members do not all share the same religion. In others, the children may not have the same biological parents. In still others, the struggle to make a living or the desire for more material things seems to force family members apart. Yet, circumstances that divide one household may not affect another. What makes the difference?

2 Viewpoint is one factor. If you sincerely try to understand the other person's point of view, you are more likely to discern how to preserve a united household. A second factor is your source of guidance. Many people follow the advice of workmates, neighbors, newspaper columnists, or other human guides. Some, though, have found out what God's Word says about their situation, and then they applied what they learned. How can doing this help a family to maintain peace in a household?—2 Timothy 3:16, 17.

---

1. What are some things that may cause divisions in families?
2. Where do some look for guidance in family life, but what is the best source of such guidance?

IF YOUR HUSBAND HAS A DIFFERENT FAITH

³ The Bible strongly counsels us against marrying someone with a different religious faith. (Deuteronomy 7:3, 4; 1 Corinthians 7:39) It may be, however, that you learned the truth from the Bible after your marriage but your husband did not. What then? Of course, the marriage vows still hold. (1 Corinthians 7:10) The Bible emphasizes the permanence of the marriage bond and encourages married people to work out their differences rather than to run away from them. (Ephesians 5:28-31; Titus 2:4, 5) What, though, if your husband strongly objects to your practicing the religion of the Bible? He may try to hinder you from going to congregation meetings, or he may say that he does not want his wife to go from house to house, talking about religion. What will you do?

⁴ Ask yourself, 'Why does my husband feel the way he does?' (Proverbs 16:20, 23) If he does not really understand what you are doing, he may worry about you. Or he may be under pressure from relatives because you no longer share in certain customs that are important to them. "Alone in the house, I felt deserted," said one husband. This man felt that he was losing his wife to a religion. Yet pride kept him from admitting that he was lonely. Your husband may need the reassurance that your love for Jehovah does not mean that you now love your husband less than you did in the past. Be sure to spend time with him.

---

3. (a) What is the Bible's counsel regarding marrying one of a different faith? (b) What are some basic principles that apply if one spouse is a believer and the other is not?
4. In what way can a wife show empathy if her husband does not share her faith?

Try to understand the other person's viewpoint

⁵ However, something even more important must be considered if you are going to deal with the situation wisely. God's Word urges wives: "Be in subjection to your husbands, as it is becoming in the Lord." (Colossians 3:18) Thus, it cautions against a spirit of independence. In addition, by saying "as it is becoming in the Lord," this scripture indicates that subjection to one's husband should also take into consideration subjection to the Lord. There has to be a balance.

⁶ For a Christian, attending congregation meetings and witnessing to others about one's Bible-based faith are important aspects of true worship that are not to be neglected. (Romans 10:9, 10, 14; Hebrews 10:24, 25) What would you do, then, if a

---

5. What balance must be kept by the wife whose husband is of a different faith?
6. What principles should be kept in mind by a Christian wife?

human directly commanded you not to comply with a specific requirement of God? The apostles of Jesus Christ declared: "We must obey God as ruler rather than men." (Acts 5:29) Their example provides a precedent that is applicable to many situations in life. Will love for Jehovah move you to render to him the devotion that rightly belongs to him? At the same time, will your love and respect for your husband cause you to try to do this in a way that is acceptable to him?—Matthew 4:10; 1 John 5:3.

7 Jesus noted that this would not always be possible. He warned that because of opposition to true worship, believing members of some families would feel cut off, as if a sword had come between them and the rest of the family. (Matthew 10:34-36) A woman in Japan experienced this. She was opposed by her husband for 11 years. He harshly mistreated her and frequently locked her out of the house. But she persevered. Friends in the Christian congregation helped her. She prayed incessantly and drew much encouragement from 1 Peter 2:20. This Christian woman was convinced that if she remained firm, someday her husband would join her in serving Jehovah. And he did.

8 There are many practical things you can do to affect your mate's attitude. For example, if your husband objects to your religion, do not give him valid causes for complaint in other areas. Keep the home clean. Care for your personal appearance. Be generous with expressions of love and appreciation. Instead of criticizing, be supportive. Show that you look to him for headship. Do not retaliate if you feel

7. What determination must a Christian wife have?
8, 9. How should a wife act to avoid putting unnecessary obstacles before her husband?

you have been wronged. (1 Peter 2:21, 23) Make allowances for human imperfection, and if a dispute arises, humbly be the first to apologize.—Ephesians 4:26.

9 Do not let your attendance at meetings be a reason for his meals being late. You may also choose to share in the Christian ministry at times when your husband is not at home. It is wise for a Christian wife to refrain from preaching to her husband when this is unwelcome. Rather, she follows the apostle Peter's counsel: "You wives, be in subjection to your own husbands, in order that, if any are not obedient to the word, they may be won without a word through the conduct of their wives, because of having been eyewitnesses of your chaste conduct together with deep respect." (1 Peter 3:1, 2) Christian wives work on more fully manifesting the fruits of God's spirit.—Galatians 5:22, 23.

WHEN THE WIFE IS
NOT A PRACTICING CHRISTIAN

10 What if the husband is the practicing Christian and the wife is not? The Bible gives direction for such situations. It says: "If any brother has an unbelieving wife, and yet she is agreeable to dwelling with him, let him not leave her." (1 Corinthians 7:12) It also admonishes husbands: "Keep on loving your wives."—Colossians 3:19.

11 If you are the husband of a wife with a faith different from yours, be especially careful to show respect for your wife and consideration for her

---

10. How should a believing husband act toward his wife if she is of a different persuasion?
11. How can a husband show discernment and tactfully exercise headship over his wife if she is not a practicing Christian?

feelings. As an adult, she deserves a measure of freedom to practice her religious beliefs, even if you disagree with them. The first time you talk to her about your faith, do not expect her to discard long-held beliefs in favor of something new. Instead of abruptly saying that practices she and her family have cherished for a long time are false, patiently endeavor to reason with her from the Scriptures. It may be that she feels neglected if you devote a great deal of time to the activities of the congregation. She may oppose your efforts to serve Jehovah, yet the basic message may simply be: "I need more of your time!" Be patient. With your loving consideration, in time she may be helped to embrace true worship.—Colossians 3:12-14; 1 Peter 3:8, 9.

TRAINING THE CHILDREN

¹² In a household that is not united in worship, religious instruction of the children sometimes becomes an issue. How should Scriptural principles be applied? The Bible assigns the father primary responsibility for instructing the children, but the mother also has an important role to play. (Proverbs 1:8; compare Genesis 18:19; Deuteronomy 11:18, 19.) Even if he does not accept the headship of Christ, the father is still the family head.

¹³ Some unbelieving fathers do not object if the mother instructs the children in religious matters. Others do. What if your husband refuses to permit you to take the children to congregation

---

12. Even if a husband and his wife are of different faiths, how should Scriptural principles be applied in the training of their children?
13, 14. If the husband forbids his wife to take the children to Christian meetings or study with them, what can she do?

meetings or even forbids you to study the Bible with them at home? Now you have to balance a number of obligations—your obligation to Jehovah God, to your husbandly head, and to your beloved children. How can you reconcile these?

¹⁴ Certainly you will pray about the matter. (Philippians 4:6, 7; 1 John 5:14) But in the end, you are the one who must decide what course to take. If you proceed with tact, making it clear to your husband that you are not challenging his headship, his opposition may eventually lessen. Even if your husband forbids you to take your children to meetings or to have a formal Bible study with them, you can still teach them. By your daily conversation and your good example, try to inculcate in them a degree of love for Jehovah, faith in his Word, respect for parents—including their father—loving concern for other people, and appreciation for conscientious work habits. In time, the father may notice the good results and may appreciate the value of your efforts. —Proverbs 23:24.

¹⁵ If you are a husband who is a believer and your wife is not, then you must shoulder the responsibility to bring up your children "in the discipline and mental-regulating of Jehovah." (Ephesians 6:4) While doing so, you should, of course, be kind, loving, and reasonable in dealing with your wife.

IF YOUR RELIGION IS NOT THAT OF YOUR PARENTS

¹⁶ It is no longer uncommon for even minor chil-

---

15. What is the responsibility of a believing father in the education of the children?
16, 17. What Bible principles must children remember if they accept a faith different from that of their parents?

dren to embrace religious views that are different from those of their parents. Have you done that? If so, the Bible has counsel for you.

¹⁷ God's Word says: "Be obedient to your parents in union with the Lord, for this is righteous: 'Honor your father and your mother.'" (Ephesians 6: 1, 2) That involves wholesome respect for parents. However, while obedience to parents is important, it must not be rendered without regard for the true God. When a child gets old enough to begin making decisions, he bears an increased measure of responsibility for his actions. This is true not only with regard to secular law but especially concerning divine law. "Each of us will render an account for himself to God," the Bible states.—Romans 14:12.

¹⁸ If your beliefs cause you to make changes in your life, try to understand your parents' point of view. They will likely be pleased if, as a result of your learning and applying Bible teachings, you become more respectful, more obedient, more diligent in what they ask of you. However, if your new faith also causes you to reject beliefs and customs that they personally cherish, they may feel that you are spurning a heritage that they sought to give you. They may also fear for your welfare if what you are doing is not popular in the community or if it diverts your attention from pursuits that they feel could help you to prosper materially. Pride could also be a barrier. They may feel that you are, in effect, saying that you are right and they are wrong.

18, 19. If children have a religion that is different from that of their parents, how can they help their parents to understand their faith better?

[19] As soon as possible, therefore, try to arrange for your parents to meet some of the elders or other mature Witnesses from the local congregation. Encourage your parents to visit a Kingdom Hall to hear for themselves what is discussed and to see firsthand what sort of people Jehovah's Witnesses are. In time, your parents' attitude may soften. Even when parents are adamantly opposed, destroy Bible literature, and forbid children to attend Christian meetings, there usually are opportunities to read elsewhere, to talk to fellow Christians, and to witness to and help others informally. You can also pray to Jehovah. Some youths have to wait until they are old enough to live outside the family home before they can do more. Whatever the situation at home, however, do not forget to "honor your father and your mother." Do your part to contribute to peace in the home. (Romans 12:17, 18) Above all, pursue peace with God.

THE CHALLENGE OF BEING A STEPPARENT

[20] In many homes the situation that presents the greatest challenge is not religious but biological. Many households today include children from previous marriages of one or both of the parents. In such a family, children may experience jealousy and resentment or perhaps a conflict of loyalties. As a result, they may rebuff the sincere efforts of the stepparent to be a good father or mother. What can help to make a stepfamily successful?

[21] Realize that in spite of the special circumstanc-

---

20. What feelings may children have if their father or mother is a stepparent?
21. Despite their special circumstances, why should stepparents look to principles found in the Bible for help?

es, Bible principles that bring success in other households apply here also. Ignoring those principles may, for the moment, seem to relieve a problem but will likely lead to heartache later. (Psalm 127:1; Proverbs 29:15) Cultivate wisdom and discernment —wisdom to apply godly principles with long-term benefits in mind, and discernment to identify why family members say and do certain things. There is also a need for empathy.—Proverbs 16:21; 24:3; 1 Peter 3:8.

22 If you are a stepparent, you may recall that as a friend of the family, you were perhaps welcomed by the children. But when you became their stepparent, their attitude may have changed. Remembering the biological parent who is no longer living with them, the children may be struggling with a conflict of loyalties, possibly feeling that you want to take away the affection that they have for the absent parent. At times, they might bluntly remind you that you are not *their* father or *their* mother. Such statements hurt. Still, "do not hurry yourself in your spirit to become offended." (Ecclesiastes 7:9) Discernment and empathy are needed in order to deal with the children's emotions.

23 Those qualities are crucial when one is administering discipline. Consistent discipline is vital. (Proverbs 6:20; 13:1) And since children are not all the same, discipline may differ from one case to another. Some stepparents find that, at least to start with, it may be better for the biological parent

---

22. Why may children find it difficult to accept a stepparent?
23. How may discipline be handled in a family with stepchildren?

*Whether a natural parent or a stepparent,
rely on the Bible for guidance*

to handle this aspect of parenting. It is essential, though, that both parents agree on the discipline and uphold it, not favoring a natural offspring over a stepchild. (Proverbs 24:23) Obedience is important, but allowances for imperfection need to be made. Do not overreact. Discipline in love.—Colossians 3:21.

²⁴ Family discussions can do much to head off trouble. These can help the family to keep in focus the most important matters in life. (Compare Philippians 1:9-11.) They can also assist each one to see how he can contribute toward attaining family goals. In addition, frank family discussions can avert moral problems. Girls need to understand

---

24. What can help to avert moral problems between members of the opposite sex in a stepfamily?

PROPER MARRIAGES BRING DIGNITY AND PEACE

In our day many men and women live together as husband and wife without any legal commitment. This is a situation that a new believer may have to deal with. In some instances the union may be approved by community or tribal custom, but it is not legal. The Bible standard, however, requires a properly registered marriage. (Titus 3:1; Hebrews 13:4) For people within the Christian congregation, the Bible also stipulates that there be just one husband and one wife in a marriage union. (1 Corinthians 7:2; 1 Timothy 3:2, 12) Conforming to this standard is a first step toward having peace in your home. (Psalm 119:165) Jehovah's requirements are not unrealistic or burdensome. What he teaches us is designed to benefit us.—Isaiah 48:17, 18.

how to dress and comport themselves around their stepfather and any stepbrothers, and boys need counsel on proper conduct toward their stepmother and any stepsisters.—1 Thessalonians 4:3-8.

²⁵ In meeting the special challenge of being a stepparent, be patient. It takes time to develop new relationships. Earning the love and respect of children with whom you have no biological bond can be a formidable task. But it is possible. A wise and discerning heart, coupled with a strong desire to please Jehovah, is the key to peace in a stepfamily. (Proverbs 16:20) Such qualities can also help you to cope with other situations.

---

25. What qualities can help keep peace in a stepfamily?

DO MATERIAL PURSUITS DIVIDE YOUR HOME?

[26] Problems and attitudes regarding material things can divide families in many ways. Sadly, some families are disrupted by arguments over money and the desire to be rich—or at least a little richer. Divisions may develop when both mates work secularly and cultivate a "my money, your money" attitude. Even if arguments are avoided, when both mates work they may find themselves with a schedule that leaves little time for each other. A growing trend in the world is for fathers to live away from their families for extended periods —months or even years—in order to earn more money than they could ever earn at home. This can lead to very serious problems.

[27] No rules can be laid down for handling these situations, since different families have to deal with different pressures and needs. Still, Bible counsel can help. For example, Proverbs 13:10 indicates that needless struggle can sometimes be avoided by "consulting together." This involves not merely stating one's own views but seeking advice and finding out how the other person looks at a matter. Further, working out a realistic budget can help to unify family efforts. Sometimes it is necessary—perhaps temporarily—for both mates to work outside the home to care for added expenses, especially when there are children or other dependents. When this is the case, the husband can reassure his wife that he still has time for her. He along with the children can lov-

26. In what ways can problems and attitudes regarding material things divide a family?
27. What are some principles that can help a family under financial pressure?

ingly help with some of the work that she might normally handle alone.—Philippians 2:1-4.

²⁸ However, keep in mind that while money is a necessity in this system of things, it does not bring happiness. It certainly does not give life. (Ecclesiastes 7:12) Indeed, overemphasis on material things can cause spiritual and moral ruin. (1 Timothy 6:9-12) How much better to seek first God's Kingdom and his righteousness, with the assurance of having his blessing on our efforts to obtain life's necessities! (Matthew 6:25-33; Hebrews 13:5) By keeping spiritual interests to the fore and by pursuing peace first of all with God, you may find that your household, though perhaps divided by certain circumstances, will become one that is truly united in the most important ways.

---

28. What reminders, if observed, will help a family to work toward unity?

> ### HOW CAN THESE BIBLE PRINCIPLES HELP...
> ### FAMILY MEMBERS TO PRESERVE
> ### PEACE IN THE HOME?
>
> ---
>
> Christians cultivate discernment.
> —Proverbs 16:21; 24:3.
>
> A couple's showing love and respect in marriage is not conditional upon their being of the same religion.—Ephesians 5:23, 25.
>
> A Christian will never deliberately break God's law.—Acts 5:29.
>
> Christians are peacemakers.—Romans 12:18.
>
> Do not take offense quickly.—Ecclesiastes 7:9.

CHAPTER TWELVE

You Can Overcome Problems That Damage a Family

THE old car has just been washed and waxed. To passersby it looks shiny, almost new. But underneath the surface, corrosive rust is eating away the body of the vehicle. It is similar with some families. Although to outward appearances everything looks fine, smiling faces hide fear and pain. Behind closed doors corrosive elements are eating away at family peace. Two problems that can have this effect are alcoholism and violence.

THE DAMAGE CAUSED BY ALCOHOLISM

² The Bible does not condemn the moderate use of alcoholic beverages, but it does condemn drunkenness. (Proverbs 23:20, 21; 1 Corinthians 6:9, 10; 1 Timothy 5:23; Titus 2:2, 3) Alcoholism, though, is more than drunkenness; it is a chronic preoccupation with alcoholic drinks and a loss of control over their consumption. Alcoholics can be adults. Sadly, they can also be youths.

³ The Bible long ago indicated that misuse of alcohol can disrupt family peace. (Deuteronomy 21: 18-21) The corrosive effects of alcoholism are felt by

---

1. What hidden problems exist in some families?
2. (a) What is the Bible's view of the use of alcoholic beverages? (b) What is alcoholism?
3, 4. Describe the effects of alcoholism on the spouse of the alcoholic and on the children.

142   FAMILY HAPPINESS

the entire family. The spouse may become absorbed in efforts to stop the alcoholic's drinking or to cope with his unpredictable behavior.* She tries concealing the liquor, throwing it away, hiding his money, and appealing to his love for family, for life, even for God—but the alcoholic still drinks. As her efforts to control his drinking meet with repeated failure, she feels frustrated and inadequate. She may begin to suffer from fear, anger, guilt, nervousness, anxiety, and lack of self-respect.

⁴ Children do not escape the effects of a parent's alcoholism. Some are assaulted physically. Others are molested sexually. They may even blame themselves for a parent's alcoholism. Frequently their ability to trust others is shattered by the alcoholic's inconsistent behavior. Because they cannot comfortably talk about what is happening at home, the children may learn to suppress their feelings, often with harmful physical consequences. (Proverbs 17:22) Such children may carry this lack of self-confidence or self-respect right into adulthood.

WHAT CAN THE FAMILY DO?

⁵ Although many authorities say that alcoholism cannot be cured, most agree that a measure of recovery is possible with a program of *total abstinence.* (Compare Matthew 5:29.) However, getting an alcoholic to accept help is easier said than done, since he usually denies that he has a problem. Nevertheless, when family members take steps to deal with the way the alcoholism has affected them,

---

* Although we refer to the alcoholic as a male, the principles herein apply equally when the alcoholic is a female.

---

5. How can alcoholism be managed, and why is this difficult?

the alcoholic may begin to realize that he has a problem. A physician with experience in helping alcoholics and their families said: "I think the most important thing is for the family simply to go about their business of living in the healthiest way they can. The alcoholic more and more gets confronted with how big the contrast is between him and the rest of the family."

6 If there is an alcoholic in your family, the Bible's inspired counsel can assist you in living in the healthiest way possible. (Isaiah 48:17; 2 Timothy 3: 16, 17) Consider some principles that have helped families to deal successfully with alcoholism.

7 *Stop taking all the blame.* The Bible says: "Each one will carry his own load," and, "each of us will render an account for himself to God." (Galatians 6:5; Romans 14:12) The alcoholic may try to suggest that family members are responsible. For example, he may say: "If you treated me better, I wouldn't drink." If others appear to agree with him, they are encouraging him to continue drinking. But even if we are victimized by circumstances or by other people, all of us—including alcoholics—are responsible for what we do.—Compare Philippians 2:12.

8 *Do not feel that you must always shield the alcoholic from the consequences of his drinking.* A Bible proverb about someone in a rage could apply equally to the alcoholic: "If you would deliver him, you will also keep doing it again and again." (Proverbs 19:19)

6. What is the best source of counsel for families with an alcoholic member?

7. If a family member is an alcoholic, who is responsible?

8. What are some ways that the alcoholic may be helped to face the consequences of his problem?

Let the alcoholic feel the effects of his drinking. Let him clean up after himself or call his employer the morning after a drinking episode.

⁹ *Accept help from others.* Proverbs 17:17 says: "A true companion is loving all the time, and is a brother that is born for when there is distress." When there is an alcoholic in your family, there is distress. You need help. Do not hesitate to rely on 'true companions' for support. (Proverbs 18:24) Talking with others who understand the problem or who have faced a similar situation may provide you with practical suggestions on what to do and what not to do. But be balanced. Speak with those you trust, those who will protect your "confidential talk." —Proverbs 11:13.

¹⁰ *Learn to trust Christian elders.* The elders in the Christian congregation can be a great source of help. These mature men are educated in God's Word and experienced in the application of its principles. They can prove to be "like a hiding place from the wind and a place of concealment from the rainstorm, like streams of water in a waterless country, like the shadow of a heavy crag in an exhausted land." (Isaiah 32:2) Not only do Christian elders protect the congregation as a whole from harmful influences but they also comfort, refresh, and take a personal interest in individuals who have problems. Take full advantage of their help.

¹¹ *Above all, draw strength from Jehovah.* The Bible warmly assures us: "Jehovah is near to those

---

9, 10. Why should the families of alcoholics accept help, and whose help in particular should they seek?
11, 12. Who provides the greatest help for families of alcoholics, and how is that support given?

Christian elders can be a great source of help in solving family problems

that are broken at heart; and those who are crushed in spirit he saves." (Psalm 34:18) If you feel broken at heart or crushed in spirit because of the pressures of living with an alcoholic family member, know that "Jehovah is near." He understands how difficult your family situation is.—1 Peter 5:6, 7.

¹² Believing what Jehovah says in his Word can help you to cope with anxiety. (Psalm 130:3, 4; Matthew 6:25-34; 1 John 3:19, 20) Studying God's Word and living by its principles puts you in line to receive the help of God's holy spirit, which can equip you with "power beyond what is normal" to cope from one day to the next.—2 Corinthians 4:7.*

---

* In some lands, there are treatment centers, hospitals, and recovery programs that specialize in helping alcoholics and their families. Whether to seek such help or not is a personal decision. The Watch Tower Society does not endorse any particular treatment. However, care must be exercised so that, in seeking help, one does not become involved in activities that compromise Scriptural principles.

¹³ Abuse of alcohol can lead to another problem that damages many families—domestic violence.

DAMAGE CAUSED BY DOMESTIC VIOLENCE

¹⁴ The first violent act in human history was an incident of domestic violence involving two brothers, Cain and Abel. (Genesis 4:8) Ever since then, mankind has been plagued with all manner of domestic violence. There are husbands who batter wives, wives who attack husbands, parents who cruelly beat their young children, and grown children who abuse their elderly parents.

¹⁵ The damage caused by domestic violence goes far beyond the physical scars. One battered wife said: "There is a lot of guilt and shame you have to deal with. Most mornings, you just want to stay in bed, hoping it was just a bad dream." Children who observe or experience domestic violence may themselves be violent when they grow up and have families of their own.

¹⁶ Domestic violence is not limited to physical abuse. Often the assault is verbal. Proverbs 12:18 says: "There exists the one speaking thoughtlessly as with the stabs of a sword." These "stabs" that characterize domestic violence include name-calling and shouting, as well as constant criticism, degrading insults, and threats of physical violence. The wounds of emotional violence are invisible and often go unnoticed by others.

---

13. What is a second problem that damages many families?
14. When did domestic violence begin, and what is the situation today?
15. How are family members affected emotionally by domestic violence?
16, 17. What is emotional abuse, and how are family members affected by it?

¹⁷ Especially sad is the emotional battering of a child—the constant criticizing and belittling of a child's abilities, intelligence, or value as a person. Such verbal abuse can destroy the spirit of a child. True, all children need discipline. But the Bible instructs fathers: "Do not be exasperating your children, so that they do not become downhearted." —Colossians 3:21.

HOW TO AVOID DOMESTIC VIOLENCE

¹⁸ Domestic violence begins in the heart and mind; the way we act begins with how we think. (James 1:14, 15) To stop the violence, the abuser needs to transform his way of thinking. (Romans 12:2) Is that possible? Yes. God's Word has the power to change people. It can uproot even "strongly entrenched" destructive views. (2 Corinthians 10:4; Hebrews 4:12) Accurate knowledge of the Bible can help produce so complete a change in people that they are said to put on a new personality.—Ephesians 4:22-24; Colossians 3:8-10.

¹⁹ *View of marriage mate.* God's Word says: "Husbands ought to be loving their wives as their own bodies. He who loves his wife loves himself." (Ephesians 5:28) The Bible also says that a husband should assign his wife "honor as to a weaker vessel." (1 Peter 3:7) Wives are admonished "to love their husbands" and to have "deep respect" for them. (Titus 2:4; Ephesians 5:33) Surely no God-fearing husband can truthfully argue that he really honors his wife if he assaults her physically or verbally. And no wife who screams at her husband, addresses him

18. Where does domestic violence begin, and what does the Bible show is the way to stop it?
19. How should a Christian view and treat a marriage mate?

sarcastically, or constantly scolds him can say that she truly loves and respects him.

[20] *Proper view of children.* Children deserve, yes, need, love and attention from their parents. God's Word calls children "an inheritance from Jehovah" and "a reward." (Psalm 127:3) Parents are responsible before Jehovah to care for that inheritance. The Bible speaks of "the traits of a babe" and the "foolishness" of boyhood. (1 Corinthians 13:11; Proverbs 22:15) Parents should not be surprised if they encounter foolishness in their children. Youngsters are not adults. Parents should not demand more than is appropriate for a child's age, family background, and ability.—See Genesis 33:12-14.

[21] *View of elderly parents.* Leviticus 19:32 says: "Before gray hair you should rise up, and you must show consideration for the person of an old man." God's Law thus fostered respect and a high regard for the elderly. This may be a challenge when an elderly parent seems overly demanding or is ill and perhaps does not move or think quickly. Still, children are reminded to "keep paying a due compensation to their parents." (1 Timothy 5:4) This would mean treating them with dignity and respect, perhaps even providing for them financially. Mistreating elderly parents physically or otherwise absolutely contradicts the way the Bible tells us to act.

[22] *Cultivate self-control.* Proverbs 29:11 says: "All

---

20. Before whom are parents responsible for their children, and why should parents not have unrealistic expectations of their children?
21. What is the godly way of viewing elderly parents and of dealing with them?
22. What is a key quality in overcoming domestic violence, and how can it be exercised?

his spirit is what a stupid one lets out, but he that is wise keeps it calm to the last." How can you control your spirit? Instead of letting frustration build up inside, act quickly to settle difficulties that arise. (Ephesians 4:26, 27) Leave the scene if you feel yourself losing control. Pray for God's holy spirit to produce self-control in you. (Galatians 5:22, 23) Going for a walk or engaging in some physical exercise may help you to control your emotions. (Proverbs 17:14, 27) Endeavor to be "slow to anger."—Proverbs 14:29.

TO SEPARATE OR REMAIN TOGETHER?

23 The Bible places among the works condemned by God "enmities, strife, . . . fits of anger" and states that "those who practice such things will not inherit God's kingdom." (Galatians 5:19-21) Therefore, anyone claiming to be a Christian who repeatedly and unrepentantly gives in to violent fits of anger, perhaps including physical abuse of spouse or children, can be disfellowshipped from the Christian congregation. (Compare 2 John 9, 10.) In this way the congregation is kept clean of abusive persons. —1 Corinthians 5:6, 7; Galatians 5:9.

24 What about Christians who are currently being battered by an abusive spouse who shows no sign of changing? Some have chosen to stay with the abusive spouse for one reason or another. Others have chosen to leave, feeling that their physical, mental, and spiritual health—perhaps even their life—is in danger. What a victim of domestic violence

---

23. What may happen if a member of the Christian congregation repeatedly and unrepentantly gives in to violent fits of anger, perhaps including physical abuse of his family?
24. (a) How may abused spouses choose to act? (b) How may concerned friends and elders support an abused spouse, but what should they not do?

Christian mates who love and respect each other will act quickly to settle difficulties

chooses to do in these circumstances is a personal decision before Jehovah. (1 Corinthians 7:10, 11) Well-meaning friends, relatives, or Christian elders may wish to offer help and counsel, but they should not put pressure on a victim to take any particular course of action. That is his or her own decision to make.—Romans 14:4; Galatians 6:5.

AN END TO DAMAGING PROBLEMS

²⁵ When Jehovah brought Adam and Eve together in marriage, he never purposed that families should

25. What is Jehovah's purpose for the family?

be corroded by damaging problems such as alcoholism or violence. (Ephesians 3:14, 15) The family was to be a place where love and peace would flourish and each member would have his mental, emotional, and spiritual needs cared for. With the introduction of sin, however, family life quickly deteriorated. —Compare Ecclesiastes 8:9.

26 Happily, Jehovah has not abandoned his purpose for the family. He promises to usher in a peaceful new world in which people "will actually dwell in security, with no one to make them tremble." (Ezekiel 34:28) At that time, alcoholism, domestic violence, and all the other problems that damage families today will be things of the past. People will smile, not to hide fear and pain, but because they are finding "exquisite delight in the abundance of peace." —Psalm 37:11.

26. What future awaits those who try to live in harmony with Jehovah's requirements?

HOW CAN THESE BIBLE PRINCIPLES HELP...
FAMILIES TO AVOID PROBLEMS THAT WOULD
CAUSE SERIOUS DAMAGE?

Jehovah condemns misuse of alcohol.
—Proverbs 23:20, 21.

Each individual is responsible for his actions.
—Romans 14:12.

Without self-control we cannot serve God
acceptably.—Proverbs 29:11.

Genuine Christians honor their elderly parents.
—Leviticus 19:32.

FAMILY HAPPINESS

CHAPTER THIRTEEN

If Marriage Is at the Breaking Point

IN 1988 an Italian woman named Lucia was very depressed.* After ten years her marriage was ending. Many times she had tried to bring about a reconciliation with her husband, but it just did not work out. So she separated because of incompatibility and now faced raising two daughters on her own. Looking back at that time, Lucia recalls: "I was certain that nothing could save our marriage."

2 If you are having marriage problems, you may be able to relate to Lucia. Your marriage may be troubled and you may be wondering if it can still be saved. If such is the case, you will find it helpful to consider this question: Have I followed all the good advice that God has given in the Bible to help make marriage a success?—Psalm 119:105.

3 When tensions are high between husband and wife, dissolving the marriage may seem to be the easiest course of action. But, while many countries have experienced a shocking rise in broken families, recent studies indicate that a large percentage of divorced men and women regret the breakup.

---

* Name has been changed.

1, 2. When a marriage is under stress, what question should be asked?

3. While divorce has become popular, what reaction is reported among many divorced persons and their families?

Handle problems quickly. Do not let the sun set with you in a provoked state

A number suffer from more health problems, both physical and mental, than do those who stay with their marriage. The confusion and unhappiness of children of divorce often last for years. Parents and friends of the broken family also suffer. And what about the way God, the Originator of marriage, views the situation?

[4] As noted in previous chapters, God purposed that marriage should be a lifelong bond. (Genesis 2:24) Why, then, do so many marriages break up? It may not happen overnight. Usually there are warning signs. Small problems in a marriage can grow bigger and bigger until they seem insurmountable. But if these problems are promptly handled with the aid of the Bible, many marital breakups could be avoided.

---

4. How should problems in a marriage be handled?

BE REALISTIC

[5] An element that sometimes leads to problems is the unrealistic expectations that one or both of the marriage partners may have. Romance novels, popular magazines, television programs, and movies can create hopes and dreams that are far removed from real life. When these dreams do not come true, a person can feel cheated, dissatisfied, even bitter. How, though, can two imperfect people find happiness in marriage? It takes work to achieve a successful relationship.

[6] The Bible is practical. It acknowledges the joys of marriage, but it also warns that those who marry "will have tribulation in their flesh." (1 Corinthians 7:28) As already noted, both partners are imperfect and are prone to sin. The mental and emotional makeup and the upbringing of each partner are different. Couples sometimes disagree about money, children, and in-laws. Insufficient time to do things together and sexual problems can also be a source of conflict.* It takes time to address such matters, but take heart! Most married couples are able to face such problems and work out mutually acceptable solutions.

DISCUSS DIFFERENCES

[7] Many find it difficult to remain calm when they discuss hurt feelings, misunderstandings, or

---

* Some of these areas were dealt with in previous chapters.

---

5. What realistic situation should be faced in any marriage?
6. (a) What balanced view of marriage does the Bible give? (b) What are some reasons for disagreements in marriage?
7, 8. If there are hurt feelings or misunderstandings between marriage partners, what is the Scriptural way of handling them?

personal failings. Instead of straightforwardly saying: "I feel misunderstood," a spouse may get emotional and exaggerate the problem. Many will say: "You only care for yourself," or, "You don't love me." Not wanting to get involved in an argument, the other spouse may refuse to respond.

⁸ A better course to follow is to heed the Bible's counsel: "Be wrathful, and yet do not sin; let the sun not set with you in a provoked state." (Ephesians 4:26) One happily married couple, on reaching their 60th wedding anniversary, were asked the secret of their successful marriage. The husband said: "We learned not to go to sleep without settling differences, no matter how minor they may have been."

⁹ When a husband and wife disagree, each one needs to "be swift about hearing, slow about speaking, slow about wrath." (James 1:19) After listening carefully, *both* partners might see the need to apologize. (James 5:16) Saying with sincerity, "Sorry for hurting you," takes humility and courage. But handling differences in this manner will go a long way in helping a married couple not only to solve their problems but also to develop a warmth and intimacy that will make them find more pleasure in each other's company.

RENDERING THE MARRIAGE DUE

¹⁰ When the apostle Paul wrote to the Corinthians, he recommended marriage 'because of the prevalence of fornication.' (1 Corinthians 7:2) The

---

9. (a) What is identified in the Scriptures as a vital part of communication? (b) What do marriage mates often need to do, even if this takes courage and humility?
10. What protection recommended by Paul to Corinthian Christians might apply to a Christian today?

world today is as bad as, or even worse than, ancient Corinth. The immoral topics that people of the world openly discuss, the immodest way they dress, and the sensual stories featured in magazines and books, on TV, and in the movies, all combine to excite illicit sexual appetites. To the Corinthians living in a similar environment, the apostle Paul said: "It is better to marry than to be inflamed with passion."—1 Corinthians 7:9.

¹¹ Therefore, the Bible commands married Christians: "Let the husband render to his wife her due; but let the wife also do likewise to her husband." (1 Corinthians 7:3) Notice that the emphasis is on giving—not on demanding. Physical intimacy in marriage is truly satisfying only if each partner is concerned about the good of the other. For example, the Bible commands husbands to deal with their wives "according to knowledge." (1 Peter 3:7) This is particularly true in giving and receiving the marriage due. If a wife is not treated tenderly, she may find it difficult to enjoy this aspect of marriage.

¹² There are times when marriage mates may have to deprive each other of the marriage due. This might be true of the wife at certain times of the month or when she is feeling very tired. (Compare Leviticus 18:19.) It may be true of the husband when he is dealing with a serious problem at work and feels emotionally drained. Such cases of temporary suspension of rendering the marriage due are best handled if both partners frankly discuss the situation and agree by "mutual consent." (1 Corinthians

---

11, 12. (a) What do the husband and wife owe to each other, and in what spirit should it be rendered? (b) How should the situation be handled if the marriage due has to be temporarily suspended?

7:5) This will prevent either partner from jumping to wrong conclusions. If, though, a wife willfully deprives her husband or if a husband deliberately fails to render the marriage due in a loving way, the partner may be left open to temptation. In such a situation, problems may arise in a marriage.

[13] Like all Christians, married servants of God must avoid pornography, which can create unclean and unnatural desires. (Colossians 3:5) They must also guard their thoughts and actions when dealing with all members of the opposite sex. Jesus warned: "Everyone that keeps on looking at a woman so as to have a passion for her has already committed adultery with her in his heart." (Matthew 5:28) By applying the Bible's counsel regarding sex, couples should be able to avoid falling into temptation and committing adultery. They can continue to enjoy delightful intimacy in a marriage in which sex is treasured as a wholesome gift from the Originator of marriage, Jehovah.—Proverbs 5:15-19.

THE BIBLICAL GROUNDS FOR DIVORCE

[14] Happily, in most Christian marriages, any problems that arise can be handled. Sometimes, though, this is not the case. Because humans are imperfect and live in a sinful world that is under the control of Satan, some marriages do reach the breaking point. (1 John 5:19) How should Christians deal with such a trying situation?

[15] As mentioned in Chapter 2 of this book, for-

---

13. How can Christians work to keep their thinking clean?
14. What sad situation sometimes presents itself? Why?
15. (a) What is the only Scriptural basis for divorce with the possibility of remarriage? (b) Why have some decided against divorcing an unfaithful marriage mate?

nication is the only Scriptural ground for divorce with the possibility of remarriage.* (Matthew 19:9) If you have definite proof that your marriage mate has been unfaithful, then you face a difficult decision. Will you continue in the marriage or get a divorce? There are no rules. Some Christians have completely forgiven a genuinely repentant partner, and the preserved marriage has turned out well. Others have decided against divorce for the sake of the children.

[16] On the other hand, the sinful act may have resulted in pregnancy or a sexually transmitted disease. Or perhaps the children need to be protected from a sexually abusive parent. Clearly, there is much to consider before making a decision. If, however, you learn of the infidelity of your marriage partner and afterward resume sexual relations with your mate, you thus indicate that you have forgiven your mate and desire to continue in the marriage. Grounds for divorce with the Scriptural possibility of remarriage no longer exist. No one should be a busybody and try to influence your decision, nor should anyone criticize your decision when you make it. You will have to live with the consequences of what you decide. "Each one will carry his own load."—Galatians 6:5.

---

* The Bible term translated "fornication" includes acts of adultery, homosexuality, bestiality, and other willful illicit acts involving use of the sex organs.

---

16. (a) What are some factors that have moved some to divorce their erring marriage mate? (b) When an innocent mate makes a decision to divorce or not to divorce, why should no one criticize that one's decision?

GROUNDS FOR SEPARATION

¹⁷ Are there situations that may justify separation or possibly divorce from a marriage mate even if that one has not committed fornication? Yes, but in such a case, a Christian is not free to pursue a third party with a view to remarriage. (Matthew 5:32) The Bible, while making allowances for such separation, stipulates that the one departing should "remain unmarried or else make up again." (1 Corinthians 7:11) What are some extreme situations that may make a separation seem advisable?

¹⁸ Well, the family may become destitute because of the gross laziness and bad habits of the husband.* He may gamble away the family's income or use it to support an addiction to drugs or alcohol. The Bible states: "If anyone does not provide for . . . members of his household, he has disowned the faith and is worse than a person without faith." (1 Timothy 5:8) If such a man refuses to change his ways, perhaps even financing his vices by taking money that his wife earns, the wife may choose to protect her welfare and that of her children by obtaining a legal separation.

¹⁹ Such legal action may also be considered if a spouse is extremely violent toward the partner, perhaps repeatedly beating that one to the extent that

---

* This does not include situations in which a husband, although well-intentioned, is unable to provide for his family for reasons beyond his control, such as sickness or lack of employment opportunities.

---

17. If there is no fornication, what limitations do the Scriptures place on separation or divorce?
18, 19. What are some of the extreme situations that may lead a spouse to weigh the advisability of legal separation or divorce, even though remarriage is not a possibility?

health and even life are in danger. Additionally, if a spouse constantly tries to force a marriage mate to break God's commands in some way, the threatened mate may also consider separation, especially if matters reach the point where spiritual life is endangered. The partner at risk may conclude that the only way to "obey God as ruler rather than men" is to obtain a legal separation.—Acts 5:29.

²⁰ In all cases of extreme spousal abuse, no one should put pressure on the innocent mate either to separate or to stay with the other. While mature friends and elders may offer support and Bible-based counsel, these cannot know all the details of what goes on between a husband and wife. Only Jehovah can see that. Of course, a Christian wife would not be honoring God's marriage arrangement if she used flimsy excuses to get out of a marriage. But if an extremely dangerous situation persists, no one should criticize her if she chooses to separate. Exactly the same things could be said concerning a Christian husband who seeks separation. "We shall all stand before the judgment seat of God." —Romans 14:10.

HOW A BROKEN MARRIAGE WAS SAVED

²¹ Three months after Lucia, mentioned earlier, separated from her husband, she met Jehovah's Witnesses and started to study the Bible with them. "To my great surprise," she explains, "the Bible supplied practical solutions to my problem. After just

---

20. (a) In the case of a family breakup, what may mature friends and elders offer, and what should they not offer? (b) Married individuals should not use the Bible's references to separation and divorce as an excuse to do what?
21. What experience shows that the Bible's counsel on marriage works?

one week of study, I immediately wanted to make up with my husband. Today I can say that Jehovah knows how to save marriages in crisis because his teachings help mates learn how to feel esteem for each other. It is not true, as some assert, that Jehovah's Witnesses divide families. In my case, exactly the opposite was true." Lucia learned to apply Bible principles in her life.

²² Lucia is not an exception. Marriage should be a blessing, not a burden. To that end, Jehovah has provided the finest source of marriage counsel ever written—his precious Word. The Bible can make "the inexperienced one wise." (Psalm 19:7-11) It has saved many marriages that were at the breaking point and has improved many others that had serious problems. May all married couples have full confidence in the marriage counsel that Jehovah God supplies. It really works!

22. In what should all married couples have confidence?

HOW CAN THESE BIBLE PRINCIPLES HELP . . .
TO AVOID THE BREAKUP OF A MARRIAGE?

Marriage is a source both of joy and of
tribulation.—Proverbs 5:18, 19;
1 Corinthians 7:28.

Disagreements should be handled immediately.
—Ephesians 4:26.

In a discussion, listening is as important as
speaking.—James 1:19.

The marriage due should be rendered
in a spirit of unselfishness and tenderness.
—1 Corinthians 7:3-5.

CHAPTER FOURTEEN

Growing Older Together

MANY changes occur as we grow older. Physical weakness saps our vigor. A look in the mirror reveals new wrinkles and a gradual loss of hair color—even of hair. We may suffer some memory failure. New relationships develop when the children marry, and again when grandchildren arrive. For some, retirement from secular work results in a different routine of life.

² In truth, advancing years can be trialsome. (Ecclesiastes 12:1-8) Still, consider God's servants in Bible times. Although they finally succumbed to death, they gained both wisdom and understanding, which brought them great satisfaction in old age. (Genesis 25:8; 35:29; Job 12:12; 42:17) How did they succeed in growing older happily? Surely it was by living in harmony with the principles that we today find recorded in the Bible.—Psalm 119:105; 2 Timothy 3:16, 17.

³ In his letter to Titus, the apostle Paul offered sound guidance to those who are getting older. He wrote: "Let the aged men be moderate in habits, serious, sound in mind, healthy in faith, in love, in endurance. Likewise let the aged women be reverent in behavior, not slanderous, neither enslaved to a

---

1, 2. (a) What changes occur as old age approaches? (b) How did godly men of Bible times find satisfaction in old age?
3. What counsel did Paul give for older men and women?

lot of wine, teachers of what is good." (Titus 2:2, 3) Heeding these words can help you to face the challenges of growing older.

ADAPT TO YOUR CHILDREN'S INDEPENDENCE

4 Changing roles call for adaptability. How true this proves to be when adult children leave home and get married! For many parents this is the first reminder that they are getting old. Though happy that their offspring have come of age, parents often worry about whether they did all they could to prepare the children for independence. And they may miss having them around the house.

5 Understandably, parents continue to concern themselves with the welfare of their children, even after the children leave home. "If I could only hear from them often, to reassure myself that they are all right—that would make me happy," said one mother. A father relates: "When our daughter left home, it was a very difficult time. It left a great gap in our family because we had always done everything together." How have these parents coped with the absence of their children? In many cases, by reaching out and helping other people.

6 When children get married, the role of the parents changes. Genesis 2:24 states: "A man will *leave* his father and his mother and he must stick to his wife and they must become one flesh." A recognition of the godly principles of headship and good order

4, 5. How do many parents react when their children leave home, and how do some adjust to the new situation?
6. What helps to keep family relationships in their proper perspective?

will help parents to keep things in their proper perspective.—1 Corinthians 11:3; 14:33, 40.

⁷ After a couple's two daughters married and moved away, the couple felt a void in their lives. At first, the husband resented his sons-in-law. But as he reflected on the principle of headship, he realized that his daughters' husbands were now responsible for their respective households. Therefore, when his daughters requested advice, he asked them what their husbands thought, and then he made sure to be as supportive as possible. His sons-in-law now view him as a friend and welcome his counsel.

⁸ What if newlyweds, while not doing anything unscriptural, fail to do what the parents think is best? "We always help them to see Jehovah's point of view," explain one couple who have married children, "but if we do not agree with a decision of theirs, we accept it and give them our support and encouragement."

⁹ In certain Asian lands, some mothers find it particularly difficult to accept their sons' independence. However, if they respect Christian order and headship, they find that friction with their daughters-in-law is minimized. One Christian woman finds that the departure of her sons from the family home has been a "source of ever-increasing gratitude." She is thrilled to see their ability to manage their new households. In turn, this has meant a lightening of the physical and mental load that she and her husband have to bear as they get older.

---

7. What fine attitude did one father cultivate when his daughters left home to get married?
8, 9. How have some parents adapted to the independence of their grown children?

As you grow older, reaffirm your love for each other

REINVIGORATING YOUR MARRIAGE BOND

[10] People react in various ways to reaching middle age. Some men dress differently in an attempt to appear younger. Many women worry about the changes that menopause brings. Sadly, some middle-aged persons provoke their mates to resentment and jealousy by flirting with younger members of the opposite sex. Godly older men, though, are "sound in mind," curbing improper desires. (1 Peter 4:7) Mature women likewise work to maintain the stability of their marriages, out of love for their husbands and a desire to please Jehovah.

[11] Under inspiration, King Lemuel recorded praise for the "capable wife" who rewards her husband "with good, and not bad, *all the days* of her life." A

10, 11. What Scriptural counsel will help people avoid some of the snares of middle age?

Christian husband will not fail to appreciate how his wife strives to cope with any emotional upset she experiences during her middle years. His love will prompt him to 'praise her.'—Proverbs 31:10, 12, 28.

¹² During the busy child-rearing years, both of you may have gladly put aside your personal desires to attend to your children's needs. After their departure it is time to refocus your married life. "When my daughters left home," says one husband, "I began courtship with my wife all over again." Another husband says: "We keep an eye on each other's health and remind each other of the need for exercise." So as not to feel lonely, he and his wife show hospitality to other members of the congregation. Yes, showing interest in others brings blessings. Moreover, it pleases Jehovah.—Philippians 2:4; Hebrews 13:2, 16.

¹³ Do not allow a communication gap to develop between you and your spouse. Talk together freely. (Proverbs 17:27) "We deepen our understanding of each other by caring and being considerate," comments one husband. His wife agrees, saying: "As we have grown older, we have come to enjoy having tea together, conversing, and cooperating with each other." Your being open and honest can help cement your marriage bond, giving it a resilience that will thwart the attacks of Satan, the marriage wrecker.

ENJOY YOUR GRANDCHILDREN
¹⁴ Grandchildren are "the crown" of the elderly.

---

12. How can couples grow closer together as the years pass?
13. What part do openness and honesty play as a couple grow older together?
14. What part did Timothy's grandmother evidently play in his growing up as a Christian?

(Proverbs 17:6) The companionship of grandchildren can truly be a delight—lively and refreshing. The Bible speaks well of Lois, a grandmother who, with her daughter Eunice, shared her beliefs with her infant grandson Timothy. This youngster grew up knowing that both his mother and his grandmother valued Bible truth.—2 Timothy 1:5; 3:14, 15.

[15] Here, then, is a special area in which grandparents can make a most valuable contribution. Grandparents, you have already shared your knowledge of Jehovah's purposes with your children. Now you can do likewise with yet another generation! Many young children thrill to hear their grandparents recount Bible stories. Of course, you do not take over the father's responsibility to inculcate Bible truths in his children. (Deuteronomy 6:7) Rather, you complement this. May your prayer be that of the psalmist: "Even until old age and gray-headedness, O God, do not leave me, until I may tell about your arm to the generation, to all those who are to come, about your mightiness."—Psalm 71:18; 78:5, 6.

[16] Sadly, some grandparents so spoil the little ones that tensions develop between the grandparents and their grown children. However, your sincere kindness may perhaps make it easy for your grandchildren to confide in you when they do not feel inclined to reveal matters to their parents. Sometimes the youngsters hope that their indulgent grandparents will side with them against their

15. With regard to grandchildren, what valuable contribution can grandparents make, but what should they avoid?
16. How can grandparents avoid being the cause of strain developing in their family?

parents. What then? Exercise wisdom and encourage your grandchildren to be open with their parents. You can explain that this pleases Jehovah. (Ephesians 6:1-3) If necessary, you may volunteer to pave the way for the youngsters' approach by speaking with their parents. Be frank with your grandchildren about what you have learned over the years. Your honesty and candor can benefit them.

ADJUST AS YOU AGE

17 As the years roll by, you will find that you cannot do all that you used to or all that you want to. How does one come to terms with the aging process? In your mind you may feel 30 years old, but a glance in the mirror betrays a different reality. Do not be discouraged. The psalmist beseeched Jehovah: "Do not throw me away in the time of old age; just when my power is failing, do not leave me." Make it your resolve to imitate the psalmist's determination. He said: "I shall wait constantly, and I will add to all your praise."—Psalm 71:9, 14.

18 Many have prepared in advance to increase their praise to Jehovah after retirement from secular work. "I planned ahead what I would do when our daughter left school," explains one father who is now retired. "I determined that I would start in the full-time preaching ministry, and I sold my business in order to be free to serve Jehovah more fully. I prayed for God's direction." If you are nearing the age of retirement, draw comfort from the declaration of our Grand Creator: "Even to one's old age I am the

17. What determination of the psalmist should aging Christians imitate?
18. How can a mature Christian make valuable use of retirement?

same One; and to one's gray-headedness I myself shall keep bearing up."—Isaiah 46:4.

¹⁹ Adapting to retirement from secular work may not be easy. The apostle Paul counseled aged men to be "moderate in habits." This calls for general restraint, not giving in to the inclination to seek a life of ease. There may be an even greater need for a routine and self-discipline after retirement than before. Be busy, then, "always having plenty to do in the work of the Lord, knowing that your labor is not in vain in connection with the Lord." (1 Corinthians 15:58) Widen out your activities to help others. (2 Corinthians 6:13) Many Christians do this by zealously preaching the good news at an adjusted pace. As you grow older, be "healthy in faith, in love, in endurance."—Titus 2:2.

HANDLING THE LOSS OF YOUR SPOUSE

²⁰ It is a sad but true fact that in the present system of things, married couples are eventually separated by death. Bereaved Christian spouses know that their loved ones are now sleeping, and they are confident that they will see them again. (John 11: 11, 25) But the loss is still grievous. How can the surviving one deal with it?*

²¹ Bearing in mind what a certain Bible character did will help. Anna was widowed after only seven

---

* For a more detailed discussion of this subject, see the brochure *When Someone You Love Dies,* published by the Watchtower Bible and Tract Society of New York, Inc.

19. What counsel is given for those who are growing old?
20, 21. (a) In the present system of things, what must eventually separate a married couple? (b) How does Anna provide a fine example for bereaved spouses?

years of marriage, and when we read of her, she was 84 years old. We can be sure that she grieved when she lost her husband. How did she cope? She rendered sacred service to Jehovah God at the temple night and day. (Luke 2:36-38) Anna's life of prayerful service was undoubtedly a great antidote to the sorrow and loneliness she felt as a widow.

²² "The biggest challenge for me has been having no partner to talk to," explains a 72-year-old woman who was widowed ten years ago. "My husband was a good listener. We would talk about the congregation and our share in the Christian ministry." Another widow says: "Although time heals, I have found it more accurate to say that it is what one does with one's time that helps one to heal. You are in a better position to help others." A 67-year-old widower agrees, saying: "A wonderful way to cope with bereavement is to give of yourself in comforting others."

VALUED BY GOD IN OLD AGE

²³ Though death takes away a beloved mate, Jehovah remains ever faithful, ever sure. "One thing I have asked from Jehovah," sang King David of old, "it is what I shall look for, that I may dwell in the house of Jehovah all the days of my life, to behold the pleasantness of Jehovah and to look with appreciation upon his temple."—Psalm 27:4.

²⁴ "Honor widows that are actually widows," urges the apostle Paul. (1 Timothy 5:3) The counsel that follows this instruction indicates that worthy

22. How have some widows and widowers coped with loneliness?
23, 24. What great comfort does the Bible give for aged ones, particularly those who have been widowed?

widows without close relatives may have needed material support from the congregation. Nevertheless, the sense of the instruction to "honor" includes the idea of valuing them. What comfort godly widows and widowers can draw from the knowledge that Jehovah values them and will sustain them! —James 1:27.

²⁵ "The splendor of old men is their gray-headedness," God's inspired Word declares. It is "a crown of beauty when it is found in the way of righteousness." (Proverbs 16:31; 20:29) Continue, then, whether married or single once again, to keep Jehovah's service first in your life. You will thus have a good name with God now and the prospect of eternal life in a world where the pains of old age will be no more.—Psalm 37:3-5; Isaiah 65:20.

---

25. What goal still remains for the elderly?

HOW CAN THESE BIBLE PRINCIPLES HELP... COUPLES AS THEY GROW OLDER?

Grandchildren are a "crown" for older folk.
—Proverbs 17:6.

Old age may bring added opportunities to serve Jehovah.—Psalm 71:9, 14.

Older ones are encouraged to be "moderate in habits."—Titus 2:2.

Bereaved spouses, although deeply grieved, can find comfort in the Bible.—John 11:11, 25.

Jehovah values faithful older ones.
—Proverbs 16:31.

CHAPTER FIFTEEN

Honoring
Our Elderly Parents

"**L**ISTEN to your father who caused your birth, and do not despise your mother just because she has grown old," counseled the wise man of long ago. (Proverbs 23:22) 'I would never do that!' you may say. Instead of despising our mothers—or our fathers—most of us feel a deep love for them. We recognize that we owe them a great deal. First of all, our parents gave us life. While Jehovah is the Source of life, without our parents we simply would not exist. Nothing we can give our parents is as precious as life itself. Then, just think of the self-sacrifice, anxious care, expense, and loving attention involved in helping a child along the path from infancy to adulthood. How reasonable it is, therefore, that God's Word counsels: "Honor your father and your mother . . . that it may go well with you and you may endure a long time on the earth"!—Ephesians 6:2, 3.

RECOGNIZING EMOTIONAL NEEDS

² The apostle Paul wrote to Christians: "Let [children or grandchildren] learn first to practice godly devotion in their own household and to keep paying a due compensation to their parents and grandparents, for this is acceptable in God's sight."

---

1. What debts do we owe our parents, and therefore how should we feel and act toward them?
2. How can grown children pay "due compensation" to their parents?

(1 Timothy 5:4) Grown children offer this "due compensation" by showing appreciation for the years of love, work, and care that their parents and grandparents spent on them. One way children can do this is by recognizing that like everyone else, older ones need love and reassurance—often desperately so. Like all of us, they need to feel valued. They need to feel that their lives are worthwhile.

³ So we can honor our parents and grandparents by letting them know that we love them. (1 Corinthians 16:14) If our parents are not living with us, we should remember that hearing from us can mean a great deal to them. A cheerful letter, a phone call, or a visit can greatly contribute to their joy. Miyo, who lives in Japan, wrote when she was 82 years of age: "My daughter [whose husband is a traveling minister] tells me: 'Mother, please "travel" with us.' She sends me their scheduled route and telephone number for each week. I can open my map and say: 'Ah. Now they are here!' I always thank Jehovah for the blessing of having such a child."

ASSISTING WITH MATERIAL NEEDS

⁴ Might honoring one's parents also involve caring for their material needs? Yes. It often does. In Jesus' day the Jewish religious leaders upheld the tradition that if a person declared that his money or property was "a gift dedicated to God," he was freed from the responsibility to use it to care for his parents. (Matthew 15:3-6) How callous! In effect, those religious leaders were encouraging people not

---

3. How can we honor parents and grandparents?
4. How did Jewish religious tradition encourage callousness toward elderly parents?

to honor their parents but to treat them with contempt by selfishly denying their needs. Never do we want to do that!—Deuteronomy 27:16.

⁵ In many lands today, government-supported social programs provide for some of the material needs of the elderly, such as food, clothing, and shelter. In addition to that, the elderly themselves may have been able to make some provision for their old age. But if these provisions run out or prove inadequate, children honor their parents by doing what they can to meet parental needs. In fact, caring for aged parents is an evidence of godly devotion, that is, one's devotion to Jehovah God, the Originator of the family arrangement.

LOVE AND SELF-SACRIFICE

⁶ Many adult children have responded to the needs of their infirm parents with love and self-sacrifice. Some have taken their parents into their own homes or have moved to be near them. Others have moved in with their parents. Frequently, such arrangements have proved to be a blessing to both parents and children.

⁷ Sometimes, though, such moves do not turn out well. Why? Perhaps because decisions are made too hastily or are based solely on emotion. "The shrewd one considers his steps," the Bible wisely cautions.

---

5. Despite provisions made by the governments of some lands, why does honoring one's parents sometimes include giving financial help?

6. What living arrangements have some made in order to care for the needs of their parents?

7. Why is it good not to act hastily in making decisions regarding elderly parents?

(Proverbs 14:15) For example, suppose that your elderly mother is having difficulty living alone and you think she might benefit by moving in with you. In shrewdly considering your steps, you might consider the following: What are her actual needs? Are there private or state-sponsored support services that offer an acceptable alternative solution? Does she want to move? If she does, in what ways will her life be affected? Will she have to leave friends behind? How might this affect her emotionally? Have you talked these things over with her? How might such a move affect you, your mate, your own children? If your mother needs care, who will provide it? Can the responsibility be shared? Have you discussed the matter with all those directly involved?

[8] Since the responsibility for care rests with all children in a family, it may be wise to hold a family conference so that all may share in making decisions. Talking to the elders in the Christian congregation or to friends who have faced a similar situation may also be helpful. "There is a frustrating of plans where there is no confidential talk," warns the Bible, "but in the multitude of counselors there is accomplishment."—Proverbs 15:22.

BE EMPATHETIC AND UNDERSTANDING

[9] Honoring our elderly parents requires empathy and understanding. As the years take their toll, old-

---

8. Whom may you be able to consult when deciding how to help your elderly parents?

9, 10. (a) Despite their advancing age, what consideration should be given to elderly ones? (b) Whatever steps a grown child takes in behalf of his parents, what should he always give them?

er ones may find it increasingly difficult to walk, eat, and remember. They may need help. Often the children become protective and try to provide guidance. But the elderly are adults with a lifetime of accumulated wisdom and experience, a lifetime of caring for themselves and making their own decisions. Their identity and self-respect may center on their role as parents and adults. Parents who feel they must hand over control of their lives to their children may become depressed or angry. Some resent and resist what they may see as efforts to rob them of their independence.

[10] There are no easy solutions to such problems, but it is a kindness to allow elderly parents to look after themselves and make their own decisions to the extent possible. It is wise not to make decisions about what is best for your parents without talking to them first. They may have lost much. Allow them to keep what they still have. You may find that the less you try to control your parents' lives, the better your relationship with them will be. They will be happier, and so will you. Even if it is necessary to insist on certain things for their good, honoring your parents requires that you afford them the dignity and respect they deserve. God's Word counsels: "Before gray hair you should rise up, and you must show consideration for the person of an old man." —Leviticus 19:32.

MAINTAINING THE RIGHT ATTITUDE

[11] Sometimes a problem that adult children face

11-13. If an adult child's relationship with his parents has not been good in the past, how can he still handle the challenge of caring for them in their advanced years?

in honoring their aged parents involves the relationship they had with their parents in earlier times. Perhaps your father was cold and unloving, your mother domineering and harsh. You may still feel frustrated, angry, or hurt because they were not the parents you wanted them to be. Can you overcome such feelings?*

[12] Basse, who grew up in Finland, relates: "My stepfather had been an SS officer in Nazi Germany. He easily lost his temper, and then he was dangerous. He beat up my mother many times in front of my eyes. Once when he was angry with me, he swung his belt and hit me in the face with the buckle. It hit me so hard that I tumbled over the bed."

[13] Yet, there was another side to the picture. Basse adds: "On the other hand, he worked very hard and did not spare himself in caring for the family materially. He never showed me fatherly affection, but I knew that he was emotionally scarred. His mother had thrown him out when he was a young boy. He grew up with his fists and entered the war as a young man. I could understand to some degree and did not blame him. When I grew older, I wanted to help him as much as I could up until his death. It was not easy, but I did what I could. I tried to be a good son to the end, and I think he accepted me as that."

[14] In family situations, as in other matters, the

---

* We are not here discussing situations in which parents were guilty of extreme abuse of their power and trust, to what may be viewed as a criminal degree.

---

14. What scripture applies in all situations, including those that arise in caring for elderly parents?

*It is unwise to make decisions
for a parent without talking to that one first*

Bible counsel applies: "Clothe yourselves with the tender affections of compassion, kindness, lowliness of mind, mildness, and long-suffering. Continue putting up with one another and forgiving one another freely if anyone has a cause for complaint against another. Even as Jehovah freely forgave you, so do you also."—Colossians 3:12, 13.

CAREGIVERS NEED CARE TOO

[15] Caring for an infirm parent is hard work, involving many tasks, much responsibility, and long hours. But the most difficult part is often emotional.

15. Why is caring for parents sometimes distressing?

It is distressing to watch your parents lose their health, memory, and independence. Sandy, who comes from Puerto Rico, relates: "My mother was the nucleus of our family. It was very painful to care for her. First she started limping; then she needed a cane, then a walker, then a wheelchair. After that it was downhill until she passed away. She developed bone cancer and needed constant care —day and night. We bathed her and fed her and read to her. It was very difficult—especially emotionally. When I realized that my mother was dying, I cried because I loved her so much."

¹⁶ If you find yourself in a similar situation, what can you do to cope? Listening to Jehovah by Bible reading and speaking to him through prayer will help you greatly. (Philippians 4:6, 7) In a practical way, make sure that you eat balanced meals and try to get adequate sleep. By doing this, you will be in a better condition, both emotionally and physically, to take care of your loved one. Perhaps you can arrange an occasional break from the daily routine. Even if a vacation is not possible, it is still wise to schedule some time for relaxation. In order to get time away, you may be able to arrange for someone else to stay with your ailing parent.

¹⁷ It is not unusual for adult caregivers to have unreasonable expectations of themselves. But do not feel guilty for what you cannot do. In some circumstances you may need to entrust your loved one to the care of a nursing home. If you are a caregiver, set reasonable expectations for yourself. You must

---

16, 17. What advice may help a caregiver to keep a balanced view of things?

FAMILY HAPPINESS

balance the needs not only of your parents but also of your children, your spouse, and yourself.

STRENGTH BEYOND WHAT IS NORMAL

18 Through his Word, the Bible, Jehovah lovingly provides guidance that can greatly aid a person in caring for aging parents, but that is not the only help he provides. "Jehovah is near to all those calling upon him," wrote the psalmist under inspiration. "Their cry for help he will hear, and he will save them." Jehovah will save, or preserve, his faithful ones through even the most difficult situations. —Psalm 145:18, 19.

19 Myrna, in the Philippines, learned this when caring for her mother, who was made helpless by a stroke. "There is nothing more depressing than to see your loved one suffer, unable to tell you where it hurts," writes Myrna. "It was just like seeing her drown little by little, and there was nothing I could do. Many times I would bend my knees and talk to Jehovah about how tired I was. I cried out like David, who beseeched Jehovah to place his tears in a bottle and remember him. [Psalm 56:8] And as Jehovah promised, he gave me the strength I needed. 'Jehovah came to be as a support for me.'"—Psalm 18:18.

20 It has been said that caring for aging parents is a "story without a happy ending." Despite even the best efforts at caregiving, older ones may die, as did Myrna's mother. But those who trust in Jehovah

---

18, 19. What promise of support has Jehovah made, and what experience shows that he keeps this promise?
20. What Bible promises help caregivers to keep optimistic, even if the one they are looking after dies?

know that death is not the end of the story. The apostle Paul said: "I have hope toward God . . . that there is going to be a resurrection of both the righteous and the unrighteous." (Acts 24:15) Those who have lost elderly parents in death take comfort in the resurrection hope along with the promise of a delightful new world of God's making in which "death will be no more."—Revelation 21:4.

21 Servants of God have deep regard for their parents, even though these may have grown old. (Proverbs 23:22-24) They honor them. In doing so, they experience what the inspired proverb says: "Your father and your mother will rejoice, and she that gave birth to you will be joyful." (Proverbs 23:25) And most of all, those who honor their elderly parents also please and honor Jehovah God.

---

21. What good results come from honoring elderly parents?

HOW CAN THESE BIBLE PRINCIPLES HELP . . . US TO HONOR OUR ELDERLY PARENTS?

We should give due compensation to parents and grandparents.—1 Timothy 5:4.

All our affairs must take place with love. —1 Corinthians 16:14.

Important decisions should never be made hastily.—Proverbs 14:15.

Elderly parents, even if sick and failing, must be respected.—Leviticus 19:32.

We will not always face the prospect of growing old and dying.—Revelation 21:4.

CHAPTER SIXTEEN

Secure a Lasting Future for Your Family

WHEN Jehovah united Adam and Eve in marriage, Adam expressed his joy by speaking the earliest recorded Hebrew poetry. (Genesis 2:22, 23) However, the Creator had more in mind than merely bringing pleasure to his human children. He wanted married couples and families to do his will. He told the first pair: "Be fruitful and become many and fill the earth and subdue it, and have in subjection the fish of the sea and the flying creatures of the heavens and every living creature that is moving upon the earth." (Genesis 1:28) What a grand, rewarding assignment that was! How happy they and their future children would have been if Adam and Eve had done Jehovah's will in full obedience!

2 Today, too, families are happiest when they work together to do God's will. The apostle Paul wrote: "Godly devotion is beneficial for all things, as it holds promise of the life now and that which is to come." (1 Timothy 4:8) A family that lives with godly devotion and that follows Jehovah's guidance as contained in the Bible will find happiness in "the life now." (Psalm 1:1-3; 119:105; 2 Timothy 3:16) Even if only one member of a family applies Bible principles, things are better than if no one does.

3 This book has discussed many Bible principles that contribute to family happiness. Likely you

1. What was Jehovah's purpose for the family arrangement?
2, 3. How can families find the greatest happiness today?

have noticed that some of them appear repeatedly throughout the book. Why? Because they represent powerful truths that work for the good of all in various aspects of family life. A family that strives to apply these Bible principles finds that godly devotion really does 'hold promise of the life now.' Let us look again at four of those important principles.

THE VALUE OF SELF-CONTROL

⁴ King Solomon said: "As a city broken through, without a wall, is the man that has no restraint for his spirit." (Proverbs 25:28; 29:11) 'Restraining one's spirit,' exercising self-control, is vital for those who want a happy marriage. Surrendering to destructive emotions, such as rage or immoral lust, will cause damage that takes years to repair—if it can be repaired at all.

⁵ Of course, no descendant of Adam can fully control his imperfect flesh. (Romans 7:21, 22) Still, self-control is a fruit of the spirit. (Galatians 5:22, 23) Hence, God's spirit will produce self-control in us if we pray for this quality, if we apply the appropriate counsel that is found in the Scriptures, and if we associate with others who manifest it and avoid those who do not. (Psalm 119:100, 101, 130; Proverbs 13:20; 1 Peter 4:7) Such a course will help us to "flee from fornication," even when we are tempted. (1 Corinthians 6:18) We will reject violence and will avoid or conquer alcoholism. And we will deal more calmly with provocations and difficult situations. May all—including children—learn to cultivate this vital fruit of the spirit.—Psalm 119:1, 2.

---

4. Why is self-control vital in a marriage?
5. How can an imperfect human cultivate self-control, and with what benefits?

A PROPER VIEW OF HEADSHIP

⁶ The second important principle is recognition of headship. Paul described the proper order of things when he said: "I want you to know that the head of every man is the Christ; in turn the head of a woman is the man; in turn the head of the Christ is God." (1 Corinthians 11:3) This means that a man takes the lead in the family, his wife is loyally supportive, and the children are obedient to their parents. (Ephesians 5:22-25, 28-33; 6:1-4) Notice, though, that headship leads to happiness only when it is handled in a proper way. Husbands who live with godly devotion know that headship is not dictatorship. They imitate Jesus, their Head. Although Jesus was to be "head over all things," he "came, not to be ministered to, but to minister." (Ephesians 1: 22; Matthew 20:28) In a similar way, a Christian man exercises headship, not to benefit himself, but to care for the interests of his wife and children. —1 Corinthians 13:4, 5.

⁷ For her part, the wife who lives with godly devotion does not compete with or seek to dominate her husband. She is happy to be supportive of him and to work with him. The Bible sometimes speaks of the wife as being "owned" by her husband, leaving no doubt that he is her head. (Genesis 20:3) Through marriage she comes under "the law of her husband." (Romans 7:2) At the same time, the Bible calls her a "helper" and a "complement." (Genesis 2:20) She supplies qualities and abilities that her

6. (a) What is the divinely established order of headship? (b) What must a man remember if his headship is to bring happiness to his family?
7. What Scriptural principles will help a wife fulfill her God-ordained role in the family?

husband lacks, and she gives him needed support. (Proverbs 31:10-31) The Bible also says that a wife is a "partner," one who works side by side with her mate. (Malachi 2:14) These Scriptural principles help a husband and a wife to appreciate each other's position and to treat each other with proper respect and dignity.

"BE SWIFT ABOUT HEARING"

⁸ In this book the need for communication is frequently highlighted. Why? Because things work better when people talk to and really listen to each other. It was repeatedly emphasized that communication is a two-way street. The disciple James expressed it this way: "Every man must be swift about hearing, slow about speaking."—James 1:19.

⁹ It is also important to be careful about *how* we speak. Rash, contentious, or severely critical words do not constitute successful communication. (Proverbs 15:1; 21:9; 29:11, 20) Even when what we say is correct, if it is expressed in a cruel, proud, or insensitive manner, it is likely to do more harm than good. Our speech should be tasteful, "seasoned with salt." (Colossians 4:6) Our words should be like "apples of gold in silver carvings." (Proverbs 25:11) Families that learn to communicate well have taken a major stride toward achieving happiness.

THE VITAL ROLE OF LOVE

¹⁰ The word "love" appears repeatedly throughout this book. Do you remember the kind of love

---

8, 9. Explain some principles that will help all in the family to improve their communication skills.
10. What kind of love is vital in marriage?

primarily referred to? It is true that romantic love (Greek, *e'ros*) plays an important part in marriage, and in successful marriages, deep affection and friendship (Greek, *phi·li'a*) grow between a husband and a wife. But even more important is the love represented by the Greek word *a·ga'pe*. This is the love that we cultivate for Jehovah, for Jesus, and for our neighbor. (Matthew 22:37-39) It is the love Jehovah expresses toward mankind. (John 3:16) How wonderful that we can show the same kind of love for our marriage mate and children!—1 John 4:19.

¹¹ In marriage this elevated love is truly "a perfect bond of union." (Colossians 3:14) It binds a couple together and makes them want to do what is best for each other and for their children. When families face difficult situations, love helps them to handle things unitedly. As a couple get older, love helps them to support and continue appreciating each other. "Love . . . does not look for its own interests. . . . It bears all things, believes all things, hopes all things, endures all things. Love never fails."—1 Corinthians 13:4-8.

¹² The marriage union is especially strong when it is sealed not just by love between marriage mates but primarily by love for Jehovah. (Ecclesiastes 4:9-12) Why? Well, the apostle John wrote: "This is what the love of God means, that we observe his commandments." (1 John 5:3) Thus, a couple should train their children in godly devotion not simply because they love their children deeply but because

---

11. How does love work for the good of a marriage?
12. Why does love for God on the part of a married couple strengthen their marriage?

THE GIFT OF SINGLENESS

Not everyone gets married. And not all married couples choose to have children. Jesus was single, and he spoke of singleness as a gift when it is "on account of the kingdom of the heavens." (Matthew 19:11, 12) The apostle Paul also chose not to get married. He spoke of both the single and the married state as 'gifts.' (1 Corinthians 7:7, 8, 25-28) Hence, while this book has for the most part discussed matters having to do with marriage and the raising of children, we should not lose sight of the potential blessings and rewards of remaining single or of being married but childless.

this is Jehovah's command. (Deuteronomy 6:6, 7) They should shun immorality not only because they love each other but chiefly because they love Jehovah, who "will judge fornicators and adulterers." (Hebrews 13:4) Even if one partner causes severe problems in a marriage, love for Jehovah will move the other to continue following Bible principles. Happy, indeed, are those families in which love for one another is cemented by love for Jehovah!

THE FAMILY THAT DOES GOD'S WILL

¹³ A Christian's whole life is centered on doing the will of God. (Psalm 143:10) This is what godly devotion really means. Doing God's will helps families to keep their eyes on the truly important things. (Philippians 1:9, 10) For example, Jesus warned: "I came to cause division, with a man against his father, and

---

13. How will a determination to do God's will help individuals to keep their eyes on the truly important things?

a daughter against her mother, and a young wife against her mother-in-law. Indeed, a man's enemies will be persons of his own household." (Matthew 10: 35, 36) True to Jesus' warning, many of his followers have been persecuted by family members. What a sad, painful situation! Still, family ties should not outweigh our love for Jehovah God and for Jesus Christ. (Matthew 10:37-39) If one endures despite family opposition, the opposers may change when they see the good effects of godly devotion. (1 Corinthians 7:12-16; 1 Peter 3:1, 2) Even if that does not happen, no lasting good is gained by ceasing to serve God because of opposition.

[14] Doing God's will helps parents to make right decisions. For example, in some communities parents tend to view children as an investment, and they count on their children to care for them in their old age. While it is right and proper for grown children to care for their aging parents, such a consideration should not make parents direct their children to a materialistic way of life. Parents do their children no favor if they bring them up to value material possessions more than spiritual things.—1 Timothy 6:9.

[15] A fine example in this regard is Eunice, the mother of Paul's young friend Timothy. (2 Timothy 1:5) Although she was married to an unbeliever, Eunice, along with Timothy's grandmother Lois, successfully raised Timothy to pursue godly devotion. (2 Timothy 3:14, 15) When Timothy was old enough, Eunice allowed him to leave home and take up

---

14. How will a desire to do God's will help parents act in the best interests of their children?
15. How was Timothy's mother, Eunice, an excellent example of a parent who did God's will?

the Kingdom-preaching work as Paul's missionary companion. (Acts 16:1-5) How thrilled she must have been when her son became an outstanding missionary! His godly devotion as an adult reflected well on his early training. Surely, Eunice found satisfaction and joy in hearing reports of Timothy's faithful ministry, even though she probably missed having him with her.—Philippians 2:19, 20.

THE FAMILY AND YOUR FUTURE

¹⁶ Jesus was raised in a godly family and, as an adult, showed a son's proper concern for his mother. (Luke 2:51, 52; John 19:26) However, Jesus' prime objective was to fulfill God's will, and for him this included opening up the way for humans to enjoy everlasting life. This he did when he offered his perfect human life as a ransom for sinful mankind.—Mark 10:45; John 5:28, 29.

¹⁷ After Jesus' death, Jehovah raised him to heavenly life and gave him great authority, eventually installing him as King in the heavenly Kingdom. (Matthew 28:18; Romans 14:9; Revelation 11:15) Jesus' sacrifice made it possible for some humans to be selected to rule with him in that Kingdom. It also opened the way for the rest of righthearted humankind to enjoy perfect life on an earth restored to paradisaic conditions. (Revelation 5:9, 10; 14:1, 4; 21: 3-5; 22:1-4) One of the greatest privileges we have today is to tell this glorious good news to our neighbors.—Matthew 24:14.

16. As a son, what proper concern did Jesus show, but what was his prime objective?
17. What glorious prospects did Jesus' faithful course open up for those who do God's will?

¹⁸ As the apostle Paul showed, living a life of godly devotion holds the promise that people can inherit those blessings in the life "which is to come." Surely, this is the very best way to find happiness! Remember, "the world is passing away and so is its desire, but he that does the will of God remains forever." (1 John 2:17) Hence, whether you are a child or a parent, a husband or a wife, or a single adult with or without children, strive to do God's will. Even when you are under pressure or are faced with extreme difficulties, never forget that you are a servant of the living God. Thus, may your actions bring joy to Jehovah. (Proverbs 27:11) And may your conduct result in happiness for you now and everlasting life in the new world to come!

18. What reminder and what encouragement are given both to families and to individuals?

HOW CAN THESE BIBLE PRINCIPLES HELP... YOUR FAMILY TO BE HAPPY?

Self-control can be cultivated.
—Galatians 5:22, 23.

With a proper view of headship, both husband and wife seek the family's best interests.
—Ephesians 5:22-25, 28-33; 6:4.

Communication includes listening.—James 1:19.

Love for Jehovah will cement a marriage.
—1 John 5:3.

Doing God's will is the most important goal for a family.—Psalm 143:10; 1 Timothy 4:8.

Would you welcome more information or a free home Bible study?

Write Watch Tower at appropriate address below.

ALASKA 99507: 2552 East 48th Ave., Anchorage. **ALBANIA:** Kutia Postare 118, Tiranë. **ARGENTINA:** C.F. Casilla de Correo 83 (Suc. 27B), 1427 Buenos Aires. **AUSTRALIA:** Box 280, Ingleburn, N.S.W. 2565. **AUSTRIA:** Postfach 67, A-1134 Vienna. **BAHAMAS:** Box N-1247, Nassau, N.P. **BARBADOS:** Fontabelle Rd., Bridgetown. **BELGIUM:** rue d'Argile-Potaardestraat 60, B-1950 Kraainem. **BELIZE:** Box 257, Belize City. **BENIN, REP. OF:** BP 06-1131, Cotonou. **BOLIVIA:** Casilla No. 1440, La Paz. **BRAZIL:** Caixa Postal 92, 18270-970 Tatuí, SP. **BULGARIA:** P.K. 353, Sofia 1000. **CAMEROON:** B.P. 889, Douala. **CANADA:** Box 4100, Halton Hills (Georgetown), Ontario L7G 4Y4. **CENTRAL AFRICAN REPUBLIC:** B.P. 662, Bangui. **CHILE:** Casilla 267, Puente Alto. **COLOMBIA:** Apartado Aéreo 85058, Bogotá 8, D.E. **COSTA RICA:** Apartado 10043, San José. **CÔTE D'IVOIRE (IVORY COAST), WEST AFRICA:** 06 B P 393, Abidjan 06. **CROATIA:** p.p. 417, HR-10 001 Zagreb. **CURAÇAO, NETHERLANDS ANTILLES:** P.O. Box 4708, Willemstad. **CYPRUS:** P.O. Box 33, CY-2550 Dhali. **CZECH REPUBLIC:** P.O. Box 90, 198 00 Prague 9. **DENMARK:** Stenhusvej 28, DK-4300 Holbæk. **DOMINICAN REPUBLIC:** Apartado 1742, Santo Domingo. **ECUADOR:** Casilla 09-01-4512, Guayaquil. **EL SALVADOR:** Apartado Postal 401, San Salvador. **ENGLAND:** The Ridgeway, London NW7 1RN. **ETHIOPIA:** P.O. Box 5522, Addis Ababa. **FIJI:** Box 23, Suva. **FINLAND:** Postbox 68, FIN-01301 Vantaa 30. **FRANCE:** B.P. 63, F-92105 Boulogne-Billancourt Cedex. **FRENCH GUIANA:** 15 rue Chawari, Cogneau Larivot, 97351 Matoury. **GERMANY:** Niederselters, Am Steinfels, D-65618 Selters. **GHANA:** Box 760, Accra. **GREECE:** P.O. Box 112, GR-322 00 Thiva. **GUADELOUPE:** Monmain, 97180 Sainte Anne. **GUAM 96913:** 143 Jehovah St., Barrigada. **GUATEMALA:** Apartado postal 711, 01901 Guatemala. **GUYANA:** 50 Brickdam, Georgetown 16. **HAITI:** Post Box 185, Port-au-Prince. **HAWAII 96819:** 2055 Kam IV Rd., Honolulu. **HONDURAS:** Apartado 147, Tegucigalpa. **HONG KONG:** 4 Kent Road, Kowloon Tong. **HUNGARY:** Cserkut u. 13, H-1162 Budapest. **ICELAND:** P.O. Box 8496, IS-128 Reykjavik. **INDIA:** Post Bag 10, Lonavla, Pune Dis., Mah. 410 401. **IRELAND:** Newcastle, Co. Wicklow. **ISRAEL:** P. O. Box 961, 61-009 Tel Aviv. **ITALY:** Via della Bufalotta 1281, I-00138 Rome RM. **JAMAICA:** Box 180, Kingston 10. **JAPAN:** 1271 Nakashinden, Ebina City, Kanagawa Pref., 243-04. **KENYA:** Box 47788, Nairobi. **KOREA, REPUBLIC OF:** Box 33 Pyungtaek P. O., Kyunggido, 450-600. **LEEWARD ISLANDS:** Box 119, St. Johns, Antigua. **LIBERIA:** P.O. Box 10-0380, 1000 Monrovia 10. **LUXEMBOURG:** B. P. 2186, L-1021 Luxembourg, G. D. **MADAGASCAR:** B. P. 511, Antananarivo 101. **MALAWI:** Box 30749, Lilongwe 3. **MALAYSIA:** 95 Bukit Beruang Heights, Jalan Bukit Beruang, 75450 Melaka. **MARTINIQUE:** Cours Campeche, Morne Tartenson, 97200 Fort de France. **MAURITIUS:** Box 54, Vacoas. **MEXICO:** Apartado Postal 896, 06002 Mexico, D. F. **MOZAMBIQUE:** Caixa Postal 2600, Maputo. **MYANMAR:** P.O. Box 62, Yangon. **NETHERLANDS:** Noordbargerstraat 77, NL-7812 AA Emmen. **NEW CALEDONIA:** B.P. 787, Nouméa. **NEW ZEALAND:** P.O. Box 142, Manurewa. **NICARAGUA:** Apartado 3587, Managua. **NIGERIA:** P.M.B. 1090, Benin City, Edo State. **NORWAY:** Gaupeveien 24, N-1914 Ytre Enebakk. **PAKISTAN:** 197-A Ahmad Block, New Garden Town, Lahore 54600. **PANAMA:** Apartado 6-2671, Zona 6A, El Dorado. **PAPUA NEW GUINEA:** Box 636, Boroko, NCD 111. **PARAGUAY:** Casilla de Correo 482, Asunción. **PERU:** Apartado 18-1055, Lima 18. **PHILIPPINES, REPUBLIC OF:** P. O. Box 2044, 1099 Manila. **POLAND:** Skr. Poczt. 13, PL-05-830 Nadarzyn. **PORTUGAL:** Apartado 91, P-2766 Estoril Codex. **PUERTO RICO 00970:** P.O. Box 3980, Guaynabo. **ROMANIA:** Str. Parfumului 22, RO-74121, Bucharest. **RUSSIA:** ul. Tankistov, 4, Solnechnoye, 189649 St. Petersburg. **SENEGAL:** B.P. 3107, Dakar. **SIERRA LEONE, WEST AFRICA:** P. O. Box 136, Freetown. **SLOVAKIA:** P.O. Box 17, 810 00 Bratislava 1. **SLOVENIA:** Poljanska cesta 77a, SLO-61000 Ljubljana. **SOLOMON ISLANDS:** P.O. Box 166, Honiara. **SOUTH AFRICA:** Private Bag X2067, Krugersdorp, 1740. **SPAIN:** Apartado postal 132, E-28850 Torrejón de Ardoz (Madrid). **SRI LANKA, REP. OF:** 711 Station Road, Wattala 0730. **SURINAME:** P.O. Box 2914, Paramaribo. **SWEDEN:** Box 5, S-732 21 Arboga. **SWITZERLAND:** P.O. Box 225, CH-3602 Thun. **TAHITI:** B.P. 7715, 98719 Taravao. **TAIWAN:** No. 3-12, 7 Lin, Shetze, Hsinwu, Taoyuan, 327. **THAILAND:** 69/1 Soi Phasuk, Sukhumvit Rd., Soi 2, Bangkok 10110. **TOGO:** B.P. 4460, Lome. **TRINIDAD AND TOBAGO, REP. OF:** Lower Rapsey Street & Laxmi Lane, Curepe. **UKRAINE:** P.O. Box 246, 290000 Lviv. **UNITED STATES OF AMERICA:** 25 Columbia Heights, Brooklyn, NY 11201-2483. **URUGUAY:** Francisco Bauzá 3372, 11600 Montevideo. **VENEZUELA:** Apartado 20.364, Caracas, DF 1020A. **WESTERN SAMOA:** P. O. Box 673, Apia. **YUGOSLAVIA, F.R.:** Milorada Mitrovića 4, YU-11 000 Belgrade. **ZAIRE, REP. OF:** B.P. 634, Limete, Kinshasa. **ZAMBIA:** Box 33459, Lusaka 10101. **ZIMBABWE:** 35 Fife Avenue, Harare.